Vegetarian Times

Vegetarian
Entertaining

From the Editors of Vegetarian Times

Menus and Recipes by Jay Solomon
Photography by Melanie Acevedo

macmillan • usa

This book is dedicated to Robert and Amy Cima,
two remarkable friends with impeccable taste, endearing wit,
and a magnanimous sense of humor.

—Jay Solomon

MACMILLAN
A Simon & Schuster Macmillan Company
1633 Broadway
New York, NY 10019

Library of Congress Cataloging-in-Publication Data

Solomon, Jay
Vegetarian times vegetarian entertaining / from the editors of
Vegetarian times ; menus and recipes by Jay Solomon ; photography by
Melanie Acevedo.
p.   cm.
Includes index.
ISBN 0-02-861324-4
1. Vegetarian cookery. 2. Entertaining. 3. Menus.
I. Vegetarian times. II. Title.
TX837.S667   1996
641.5'636—dc20   96-18465
CIP

Manufactured in the United States of America

10 9 8 7 6 5 4 3 2 1

Book design by Nick Anderson

Acknowledgments

The editors of *Vegetarian Times* would like to thank Jay Solomon for creating the inventive and delicious menus contained in this book. Jay is every editor's dream: a truly talented and creative writer and recipe developer whose delightful personality and professional manner make working with him a pure pleasure.

Thanks also to Terry Christofferson, our tireless editorial assistant and queen of the nutrition software, who never failed to go the extra mile (usually at a run). And to Justin Schwartz, our editor at Macmillan, for his patient handling of this project.

Finally, thanks go to Toni Apgar, editorial director of *Vegetarian Times*, and to Steve Lehman, publishing director, whose foresight got this book off the ground, and who trusted me to take it from there.

—Carol Wiley Lorente
Special Projects Editor
Vegetarian Times

Contents

Introduction

Entertaining at home is one of life's finest pleasures. The sharing of fine food and friendly conversation is a universally cherished endeavor. Whether it is a casual barbecue or an elaborate formal affair, the dinner party beckons with a promise of good times, nourishing dishes, and memorable moments.

Vegetarian Times Vegetarian Entertaining offers an appealing array of inspired menus designed for entertaining at home. Here are complete full-course menus for almost every dining occasion, from festive holiday feasts and seasonal celebrations to stylish theme dinners and relaxed gatherings. The following pages abound with savory soups and salads, alluring main courses, stellar side dishes, and grand finale desserts.

An all-vegetarian dinner party naturally fits in with the growing and widespread emphasis on eating more healthful, nutrient-rich foods. Once meat is removed from the equation, a whole range of dynamic culinary possibilities opens up. The menus include a cornucopia of hearty grains, pastas, seasonal vegetables, and legumes. An abundance of fresh and dried herbs, garlic, and chile peppers accent the dishes with vibrant and refreshing tastes. In the spirit of eating well, many of the menus are low in fat, high in nutrients, and free of cream and butter.

Of course, many people greet the prospect of entertaining with mixed emotions. At the outset there are feelings of giddy anticipation and excitement. As the big day approaches, an underlying sense of responsibility looms in the air. Suddenly, the thought of hosting a dinner party reverberates with intimidation. Merely surviving the dinner becomes the operative goal. However, once a little planning and advance preparation is undertaken, hope and enthusiasm return to the forefront.

Vegetarian Times Vegetarian Entertaining is your blueprint for successful home entertaining with vegetarian cuisine. Every menu is prefaced with a preparation schedule, serving suggestions, buying tips, and useful morsels of information. Here is vivid proof that one does not have to hire a caterer to throw a stress-free dinner party or rely on hackneyed meat-based entrées. All one needs is a penchant for healthy and delectable food, a modicum of social skills, time for planning and preparation, and a desire to have fun.

Elements of Successful Entertaining

The aspiring dinner host must wear many hats: chief organizer, menu planner, shopper, cook, maître d', and social catalyst. As such, it is paramount that the host have a script or plan of action in mind. A dinner party is similar to a theatrical production and, like a play, the event can be divided into three main acts: planning, preparation, and presentation.

Act I: Planning

To both experienced chefs and novice cooks, proper planning is the hallmark of a memorable dinner party. Planning involves asking (and answering) a lot of questions. Whom will you invite? What kind of menu do you wish to serve? What date is free on the calendar? Will it be a relaxed or formal event? With or without drinks? Planning explores the rudimentary details.

Once these questions have been answered, the process has been set in motion. Mark your calendar and proceed with the invitations. In today's busy world, it is sound protocol (and common courtesy) to invite your guests at least two weeks ahead of time. Assemble a list of those who can attend.

Once the guest list is settled, browse through recipes and decide on a menu. At this point, *Vegetarian Times Vegetarian Entertaining* becomes your new best friend. Here you will find menus for almost every occasion, holiday, mood, and season. Peruse the pages; perhaps a holiday celebration, seasonal feast, or theme night will strike a chord.

These days almost every ingredient can be found throughout the year, although some may require a visit to an ethnic or specialty market. Keep in mind, however, that it is next to impossible to serve a pumpkin soup in June, a time when pumpkins are scarce and hard to find. Likewise, a fresh tomato salad in January is bound to disappoint when the only available fruits are square and rubbery. (But a soup brimming with canned stewed tomatoes can be sublime.) When choosing a menu, consider what is available and appropriate for the time of year.

Once you've chosen a menu, compile a shopping list. Depending on your schedule and propensity for grocery shopping, this task can be accomplished over a few stages. Plan to pick up pantry staples and ingredients for do-ahead recipes at least ten to fourteen days ahead of time. Shop for fresh vegetables, fruits, and herbs one or two days ahead of time. The morning of the meal is the time to buy fresh bread and flowers.

Incidentally, about one week before the dinner, take an inventory of the dining room and settings. Examine your dishware, silverware, glasses, dessert plates, and soup bowls. Decide on a tablecloth, centerpiece, and style of napkins. Do you have enough place settings? The dinner theme may offer creative ways to decorate the dining room or set the table. Now is the time to act on your inspirations.

Act II: Preparation

Advance preparation is the linchpin in your effort to host a successful dinner party. Every big meal is made up of several small acts of peeling, chopping, slicing, and dicing—tasks that can be done well ahead of time. The more food preparation accomplished in the hours (and sometimes days) before the event, the smoother the ride will be.

Before the first onion is chopped and clove of garlic peeled, the recipes must be organized into a list of kitchen tasks. A basic checklist will also optimize your time spent in the kitchen. For example, if a dish is baking in the oven or simmering for one hour, plan to work on another aspect of the meal during the cooking time. Toward this end, every menu in *Vegetarian Times Vegetarian Entertaining* offers Kitchen Countdown, a timetable filled with do-ahead suggestions for preparing and serving the meal.

In general, a great deal can be accomplished in the one or two days leading up to the meal. Soups, stews, and chilies can be made and refrigerated; vinaigrettes and dips can be blended and chilled; desserts can often be prepared. You can also chill the wines and cold beverages well ahead of time.

The morning of the dinner party (and up to several hours before), salad greens and raw vegetables can be washed and crisped in the refrigerator. The dining room can be readied, place settings arranged, and tables and chairs set up. Baked goods, such as muffins, cookies, and sweet breads, can be prepared.

Plan to be in the kitchen for at least two to three hours before dinnertime. This is the time to simmer, roast, sauté, and reheat. About thirty minutes before, set out the appetizers and dips, finish the dishes that are still "works-in-progress," and prepare any garnishes.

Timing is a key element—most likely, you want the hot dishes to finish at the same time. Most grain dishes, legume dishes, and sauces will keep warm on the stovetop (if covered) for fifteen to thirty minutes before the meal is served. If there is a dish you have reservations about and are not sure about the length of cooking time, it is a good idea to test it beforehand. If you have made a dish before, most likely you'll make it faster the second time. Temperatures are also important—always serve hot dishes on hot or warm plates and cold dishes on cold plates.

There is a time and a place for spontaneous behavior, but a dinner party is not one of them. Thinking, planning, and preparing ahead of time will make a world of difference.

Act III: Presentation

Finally, the big moment arrives. It is opening night in the kitchen; the fruition of your earnest planning and preparation is at hand. Doorbells are ringing, guests are arriving, and pleasantries are being exchanged. Dinner is about to commence. Put on your happy face!

Relax. Guests do not expect to eat as soon as they arrive. Allow time for drinks and chitchat. This is the time to serve appetizers such as guacamole, salsa, and other dips and small bites. Explain to your guests (with some fanfare) what the menu holds in store for them. On this day, you are both owner and guest of your favorite restaurant.

After the guests are seated at the table, let the dinner begin. The first course, such as a soup or salad, begins the meal. After the first course, if serving restaurant style, assemble the dinner plates in the kitchen and serve guests individually at the table. If offering a family style meal, pass the platters at the table. If serving the meal buffet style, place all of the entrées on a serving table and form a line. During the meal, attend to your guests' needs, but do not hover. Sit down at the table and enjoy the meal.

When everyone has finished the main course, clear all of the plates and silverware and make preparations for dessert. It is a good idea to offer a choice of beverages, such as coffee, tea, or aperitifs with dessert. Remember to serve the dessert with new silverware; you might also consider a change of setting and adjourn to another room.

Aside from serving a delicious meal, there are several other ways to keep your guests in the comfort zone. The temperature of the dining room should be neither too hot nor too cold. The place settings should not be too close (don't cram your guests together) or too far apart (no need to shout).

Choose background music that will complement the menu, but set the volume so it does not inhibit comfortable conversation. Consider the lighting: If it is too bright, the guests will not be flattered. Conversely, if it is too dim, a somber and drowsy mood may ensue. Try a combination of candles and lights.

Remember, entertaining should be—and can be—an enjoyable and immensely satisfying endeavor. If you have done your homework, good things will happen. Carry yourself with an air of confidence and *joie de vivre*, and the dinner guests will appreciate your efforts. *Happy entertaining!*

the Menus

a Taste of First Night

Sun-Dried Tomato Hummus with Pita • Sweet Potato Dal • Spinach Feta Pies • Confetti Quinoa Salad • Roasted Eggplant and Cucumber Dip • Cranberry Pumpkin Bread

recipes make 6 to 8 servings

Spinach Feta Pies (page 7) and Sun-Dried Tomato Hummus (page 6)

First Night is a winter festival held in towns and cities throughout North America on New Year's Eve. Communities ring in the New Year with romp, pomp, and circumstance. Main streets come alive with parades, art showings, outdoor theater and concerts, open skating, puppet shows, and wintry activities galore. It is an unbridled celebration of community art, spirit, and civic pride—a healthy (nonalcoholic) alternative to stuffy parties and smoky bars.

After a day (or night) of trooping about in winter's wonderland, most of us yearn for wholesome, replenishing fare. This First Night menu features a grazing buffet of small but fulfilling bites with big vibrant flavors sure to pique the palate. For starters, there is rustic-looking Sun-Dried Tomato Hummus with Pita, an imaginative variation on the familiar hummus theme. A well-made hummus is always a crowd pleaser, and when you give it a creative twist, it is appreciated all the more.

For a fanciful finger food, Spinach Feta Pies, savory Greek pies stuffed with spinach and feta cheese, fill the bill. Unlike spanakopita— a standard holiday appetizer made with phyllo dough and saturated with butter and fat—these individual savory morsels can be made quickly and easily with prepared bread dough. Also appearing on this stage of First Night bites is an earthy, curry-scented Sweet Potato Dal, an Indian puréed stew offering long-lasting sustenance and toasty flavors. The secret to a well-cooked dal is patience. Cook the lentils until they reach a thick, porridgelike consistency; they should be soft, not crunchy, when they are eaten.

Served along with the dal is Roasted Eggplant and Cucumber Dip, a soothing condiment for vegetables and pita and a natural companion for curry dishes. Roasted eggplant forms the foundation of a variety of dips and condiments throughout the Middle East. Once cooked and peeled, eggplants develop a creamy texture and are a perfect medium for dipping.

A Confetti Quinoa Salad, a light grain salad brimming with corn, peas, and roasted sweet peppers, provides a colorful contrast on the table. (Remember to rinse the quinoa thoroughly before preparing the salad to wash away the natural, bitter-tasting resin that coats the grains.)

Filling out the menu is Cranberry Pumpkin Bread, a moist treat radiant with flavors of the season. After days of indulging in pies, cookies, and other decadent desserts throughout the holidays, this savory bread promises a welcome reprieve from confection overload.

Kitchen Countdown

3 to 4 hours before	Make the Cranberry Pumpkin Bread.
3 hours before	Make the Roasted Eggplant and Cucumber Dip.
3 hours before	Make the Confetti Quinoa Salad and refrigerate.
2 hours (and up to 1 day) before	Prepare the Sun-Dried Tomato Hummus with Pita and refrigerate.
1½ hours before	Make the Sweet Potato Dal.
30 minutes before	Bake the Spinach Feta Pies.
Dinnertime	Transfer the dishes to serving bowls and arrange on a large serving table. Serve the entire menu as a casual buffet.
What guests can bring	Party favors and champagne, of course. (In the true spirit of First Night, however, it should be nonalcoholic champagne.)

Sun-Dried Tomato Hummus with Pita

1 cup sun-dried tomatoes (not oil-packed variety)
Two 15-ounce cans chickpeas (garbanzo beans), drained
1 cup low-fat or nonfat plain yogurt
$^1/_2$ cup tahini (sesame seed paste)
2 or 3 cloves garlic, minced
1 teaspoon ground cumin
$^1/_2$ teaspoon salt
$^1/_2$ teaspoon freshly ground black pepper
Juice of 2 lemons
2 or 3 tablespoons minced fresh parsley
4 to 6 pita breads, cut into triangles

In a medium mixing bowl, soak the tomatoes in plenty of warm water for about 1 hour. Drain the liquid and mince the tomatoes.

Combine all of the ingredients except the parsley and pita in a blender or food processor fitted with a steel blade, and process until smooth, about 5 to 10 seconds. (For a chunky hummus, mash the ingredients by hand in a mixing bowl.) Transfer the hummus to a serving bowl and refrigerate for at least 2 hours before serving.

Garnish with the parsley and serve as a dip with pita bread wedges.

Makes about 5 cups

Per $^1/_4$ Cup Hummus with $^1/_2$ Pita: 196 Calories; 7g Protein; 4g Fat; 31g Carbohydrates; 1mg Cholesterol; 369mg Sodium; 6g Fiber.

Sweet Potato Dal

1$^1/_2$ tablespoons canola oil
1 medium yellow onion, finely chopped
2 cloves garlic, minced
$^1/_2$ teaspoon turmeric
$^1/_2$ teaspoon ground cumin
$^1/_2$ teaspoon ground coriander or garam masala (see Helpful Hint)
$^1/_4$ teaspoon freshly ground black pepper

1 cup green or red lentils, rinsed
4 cups water
2 cups peeled, diced sweet potatoes
$^1/_2$ teaspoon salt
4 to 6 rounds of chapati, roti, naan (Indian flat bread), or flour tortillas (See Helpful Hint)

Helpful Hint:

Garam masala is an aromatic spice mixture available in the spice section of natural food stores, Indian markets, and some supermarkets. Indian flat breads can also be found in Indian grocery stores.

In a large saucepan, heat the oil over medium heat. Add the onion and garlic and cook, stirring, for 4 minutes. Stir in the turmeric, cumin, coriander or *garam masala*, and pepper and cook for 1 minute more. Stir in the lentils and water and cook uncovered over medium-low heat for 15 minutes, stirring occasionally.

Stir in the sweet potatoes and cook, stirring occasionally, until the lentils are tender, about 30 to 40 minutes more. Stir in the salt.

Transfer to a large serving bowl. Serve with Indian flat bread or flour tortillas.

Makes about 4 cups

Per 1/4 Cup with Bread: 130 Calories; 5g Protein; 2g Fat; 23g Carbohydrates; 0mg Cholesterol; 114mg Sodium; 4g Fiber.

Spinach Feta Pies

10-ounce package fresh spinach
1 tablespoon olive oil
1 medium yellow onion, finely chopped
2 cloves garlic, minced
1/4 cup water
1/2 teaspoon freshly ground black pepper
1 pound chilled bread dough or pizza dough, prepared or homemade
2 or 3 ounces (1/2 cup) crumbled feta cheese

Preheat the oven to 375° F.

Rinse the spinach under cold running water and remove the stems. Pat the spinach dry and coarsely chop the leaves.

In a medium saucepan, heat the oil over medium heat. Add the onion and garlic and cook, stirring, for 2 to 3 minutes. Add the spinach, water, and pepper and cook over medium heat, stirring frequently, until the spinach is wilted, about 2 to 3 minutes. Remove pan from heat and let cool slightly. Drain the excess liquid from pan. (If it cools enough, gently squeeze the spinach like a sponge over a colander.)

On flat work surface, form the dough into 8 equal balls. Roll each ball into a thin flat circle about 4 inches in diameter. Place 1 heaping table-spoon of the spinach mixture and 1 teaspoon of feta cheese in the center of each round. Fold the dough over the top and seal the edges with the back of a fork, forming a crescent-shaped pocket. Place the pies on a lightly greased baking sheet and bake until golden brown, about 11 to 13 minutes.

Remove from the oven and let cool for a few minutes before serving.

Makes 8 pies

Per Serving: 181 Calories; 7g Protein; 4g Fat; 30g Carbohydrates; 6mg Cholesterol; 337mg Sodium; 3g Fiber.

Confetti Quinoa Salad

1 1/2 cups quinoa, rinsed and drained
3 cups water
3 cups hot water
2 cups corn, fresh or frozen
1 cup frozen green peas (about half of a 10-ounce package)
3 or 4 whole scallions, trimmed and chopped
1/2 cup diced roasted sweet red pepper
2 cloves garlic, minced

3 tablespoons canola oil
1 1/2 tablespoons balsamic vinegar or red wine vinegar
2 tablespoons chopped fresh parsley
1 1/2 teaspoons Dijon mustard
1/2 teaspoon salt
3/4 teaspoon freshly ground black pepper
Leafy salad greens (such as green leaf or romaine lettuce)

In a medium saucepan, combine the quinoa and 3 cups water and bring to a simmer. Cover and cook over low to medium heat until all of the water is absorbed, about 15 minutes. Fluff with a fork and set aside for 5 minutes.

In another saucepan, bring 3 cups hot water to a simmer. Add the corn and peas and cook over medium heat, stirring occasionally, for 6 to 8 minutes. Drain and set aside until the quinoa is done.

Combine all of the ingredients except leafy greens in a large mixing bowl. Refrigerate for 3 to 4 hours before serving. Serve the salad in a bowl lined with leafy greens.

Makes 6 sevings

Per Serving: 290 Calories; 10g Protein; 10g Fat; 44g Carbohydrates; 0mg Cholesterol; 220mg Sodium; 7g Fiber.

Roasted Eggplant and Cucumber Dip

16 ounces low-fat or nonfat plain yogurt
1 medium cucumber, finely chopped (peeled if waxed)
2 to 4 scallions, whole, trimmed and chopped
2 tablespoons minced fresh cilantro
Juice of 1 lemon
1 teaspoon ground cumin
1/4 teaspoon salt
1/8 teaspoon cayenne pepper
2 medium eggplants (about 2 pounds), cut in half lengthwise
Crudités or pita bread

Preheat the broiler.

Combine the yogurt, cucumber, scallions, cilantro, lemon juice, cumin, salt, and cayenne in a mixing bowl. Set aside.

Prick the eggplants with a fork a couple of times. Arrange the eggplants cut-side down on a lightly greased baking sheet. Place the eggplants beneath the broiler and roast until the skin is charred and the flesh is tender, about 8 to 12 minutes. Remove from the heat and let cool slightly.

Scrape or peel off the charred skin and discard. Chop and mash the flesh and then fold into the yogurt mixture. Transfer the dip to a serving bowl and refrigerate for at least 2 hours before serving.

Serve with raw carrots, celery, and other assorted vegetables, such as broccoli or cauliflower florets. Pita bread can also be used to scoop up this dip.

Makes about 5 cups

Per ¼ Cup: 30 Calories; 2g Protein; 2g Fat; 5g Carbohydrates; 1mg Cholesterol; 45mg Sodium; 1g Fiber.

Cranberry Pumpkin Bread

1 cup 1% milk or soy milk	½ to 1 cup diced walnuts
½ cup canola oil	2 cups unbleached white flour
½ cup brown sugar	½ cup rolled oats (old-fashioned, not quick-cooking)
½ cup molasses	
1 large egg plus 1 egg white	2½ teaspoons baking powder
2 cups mashed pumpkin (one 14-ounce can)	1 teaspoon ground allspice or cinnamon
2 cups cranberries, fresh or frozen and thawed	1 teaspoon ground nutmeg
	1 teaspoon salt

Preheat the oven to 375° F.

In a medium mixing bowl, whisk together the milk, oil, sugar, molasses, egg, and egg white until fully incorporated. Stir in the pumpkin, cranberries, and nuts.

In a separate bowl, mix together the remaining dry ingredients. Gently fold the dry ingredients into the wet batter until fully incorporated. Spoon the batter into 2 lightly greased 9 × 5–inch loaf pans and bake until a toothpick inserted in the center comes out clean, about 45 to 50 minutes.

Remove from the oven and let stand for 15 to 30 minutes on a rack. Cover the bread until ready to serve.

Makes 2 loaves, about 12 slices per loaf

Per Slice: 152 Calories; 3g Protein; 6g Fat; 21g Carbohydrates; 12mg Cholesterol; 152mg Sodium; 2g Fiber.

a
Valentine's
Day
Soiree

Artichokes with Rouille à la Provençale • Beet and Watercress Bisque • Exotic Greens with Kiwi-Honey Vinaigrette • Bow-Tie Pasta with Wild Mushrooms and Fresh Tomato Sauce • Chocolate-Dipped Strawberries Coated with Hazelnuts

recipes make *2* servings

Artichokes with Rouille à la Provençale (page 14), Beet and Watercress Bisque (page 15), and Chocolate-Dipped Strawberries Coated with Hazelnuts (page 17)

*A*lthough Valentine's Day falls on February 14, the halo of romance encircles the entire month. Valentine's Day rescues February from the cold weather doldrums and provides excitement and intrigue for winter-weary souls. As long as there is a Valentine's Day on the calendar, romance will never die.

This Valentine's dinner promises to seduce the appetite with sultry and adventurous flavors. This feast begins with Artichokes with Rouille à la Provençale, a roasted sweet pepper sauce redolent with the perfume of garlic. The artichoke leaves are dipped into the sauce one at a time; every bite is savored. Roasting the bell peppers gives them a soft texture and smoky flavor. Add the jalapeño pepper if you like your food with a kick.

The artichoke ritual is followed by Beet and Watercress Bisque, a stunning magenta-hued soup endowed with herbal nuances and a sophisticated presence.

Love is often unpredictable and so are some of the best meals. In the middle of this epicurean performance comes Exotic Greens with Kiwi-Honey Vinaigrette, a salad designed to entice the palate with light, fruity flavors.

Then comes the pièce de résistance: Bow-Tie Pasta with Wild Mushrooms and Fresh Tomato Sauce. It is fitting that tomatoes, once called *pomme d'amour* ("the apple of love") in French, play a role in a meal with Cupid hovering about. Fresh tomato sauce has an untamed quality to it and is much more wholesome and rustic than conventional commercial sauces. The wild mushrooms give this sauce an earthy resonance with uncommonly good flavors. For a change of pace, feta cheese makes a tasty topping.

The Valentine's feast culminates in Chocolate-Dipped Strawberries Coated with Hazelnuts, a divine treat sure to inspire love at first bite. Large strawberries are both aesthetically pleasing and a pleasure to devour, especially when dipped in melted chocolate and rolled in chopped nuts.

Overall, the menu makes the most of do-ahead opportunities, leaving you time to enjoy the company as well as the food. An intimate dinner enjoyed at home can be far more rewarding than a night spent out in the midst of jostling crowds, noisy traffic, and overbooked restaurants.

Kitchen Countdown

1 day before	Make the Beet and Watercress Bisque and Kiwi-Honey Vinaigrette for the salad and refrigerate.
3 to 4 hours before	Make the rouille for the Artichokes with Rouille à la Provençale and refrigerate. Toss the salad and refrigerate.
1½ hours before	Dip the strawberries in chocolate for the dessert. Store in the refrigerator.
1 hour before	Cook the artichokes.
30 minutes before	Make the wild mushroom sauce for the Bow-Tie Pasta. Reheat the bisque.
15 to 20 minutes before	Cook the bow-tie pasta.
Dinnertime	Serve the Artichokes with Rouille à la Provençale as the first course, followed by the Beet and Watercress Bisque, then the Exotic Greens with Kiwi-Honey Vinaigrette. Keep the Bow-Tie Pasta with Wild Mushrooms and Fresh Tomato Sauce warm on the stovetop. Just before serving, top the pasta with sauce and cheese. After a brief respite, bring out the Chocolate-Dipped Strawberries Coated with Hazelnuts with champagne or coffee.
What your guest can bring	Roses, champagne, and chocolate are welcome, but not necessarily in that order.

Artichokes with Rouille à la Provençale

2 red bell peppers
2- to 3-inch slice of thick French or Italian bread, top crust removed
1 jalapeño pepper, seeded and minced (optional)
¹/₄ to ¹/₃ cup olive oil
2 cloves garlic, minced
1 teaspoon fresh lemon juice
¹/₄ teaspoon salt
2 whole artichokes, stems removed

Preheat the broiler. Roast the red bell peppers: Place peppers on a pan under the hot broiler until the skins are charred, about 5 to 7 minutes, turning after 3 or 4 minutes. Remove from the oven and let cool slightly. With a butter knife or your hands, peel off the outside skins and discard. Cut the peppers in half and remove the seeds. Chop the peppers and set aside.

Soak the bread in warm water for about 5 seconds. Gently squeeze the excess water out of the bread like a sponge. Combine the bread, jalapeño and roasted peppers, oil, garlic, lemon juice, and salt in a blender or food processor fitted with a steel blade and process until smooth, about 5 to 10 seconds. Transfer the sauce to a storage container and refrigerate until ready to serve.

Slice off about 1 inch of the top of the artichokes and discard. Place the artichokes in boiling water to cover. Cook over medium heat until the artichoke bottoms are easily pierced with a fork, about 35 to 45 minutes. Remove the artichokes with tongs and place them upside down in a colander to drain.

To serve, place each artichoke in a small bowl. Pour the rouille into a dipping bowl to be shared. Remove artichoke leaves one at a time with your fingers and dip into rouille.

Makes *2* servings

Per Serving with ¹/₃ Cup Sauce: 215 Calories; 5g Protein; 15g Fat; 20g Carbohydrates; 0mg Cholesterol; 270mg Sodium; 5g Fiber.

Beet and Watercress Bisque

1 tablespoon canola oil	$^{1}/_{4}$ cup dry red wine
1 medium red onion, diced	2 teaspoons dried parsley
1 celery stalk, chopped	1 teaspoon dried thyme
2 cloves garlic, minced	$^{1}/_{2}$ teaspoon salt
2 cups diced beets (3 to 4 beets)	$^{1}/_{2}$ teaspoon freshly ground black pepper
1 medium white potato, diced	2 cups watercress leaves (loosely packed)
4 cups water	$^{1}/_{4}$ cup low-fat or nonfat plain yogurt

In a large saucepan, heat the oil over medium heat. Add the onion, celery, and garlic and cook, stirring, for 5 minutes.

Add the beets, potato, water, wine, parsley, thyme, salt and pepper, and bring to a simmer. Cook uncovered over medium-low heat, stirring occasionally, until the beets are tender, about 35 to 40 minutes. Stir in the watercress and cook for 5 minutes more. Remove from heat and let the soup stand for about 10 minutes.

Transfer the soup to a blender or food processor fitted with a steel blade and purée. Return to the pan and keep hot, or refrigerate and reheat later.

To serve, ladle the soup into bowls and spoon a dollop of yogurt into the center. Garnish with any extra sprigs of watercress.

Makes *2* servings

Per Serving: 281 Calories; 7g Protein; 8g Fat; 44g Carbohydrates; 2mg Cholesterol; 724mg Sodium; 7g Fiber.

Exotic Greens with Kiwi-Honey Vinaigrette

Dressing

2 kiwi fruits, peeled and coarsely chopped
3 tablespoons canola oil
2 tablespoons red wine vinegar or apple cider vinegar
1 tablespoon honey
$^{1}/_{4}$ teaspoon salt
$^{1}/_{4}$ teaspoon white pepper

Salad

8 ounces mixed gourmet greens, such as radicchio, endive, romaine, or red leaf lettuce
8 cherry tomatoes, halved
$^{1}/_{2}$ cucumber, sliced (peeled if waxed)
1 large carrot, peeled and shredded

To make the dressing, combine all dressing ingredients in a blender or food processor fitted with a steel blade and process until smooth, about 5 to 10 seconds. Pour into a serving container and refrigerate until ready to use.

(continues)

To make the salad, arrange the greens, tomatoes, cucumber, and carrot on 2 salad plates. Spoon dressing over the top of each salad.

Makes *2* servings

Per Serving with 1 Tablespoon Dressing: 100 Calories; 3g Protein; 4g Fat; 17g Carbohydrates; 0mg Cholesterol; 73mg Sodium; 5g Fiber.

Bow-Tie Pasta with Wild Mushrooms and Fresh Tomato Sauce

1 tablespoon olive oil
2 cloves garlic, minced
1 small zucchini, cut in half lengthwise and sliced crosswise into thin crescents
2 ounces cremini or Italian mushrooms, sliced
2 ounces oyster mushrooms, sliced
1 small portobello mushroom cap, sliced
4 large ripe tomatoes, diced

1 teaspoon oregano
1 teaspoon basil
$1/2$ teaspoon salt
$1/2$ teaspoon freshly ground black pepper
$1/2$ teaspoon sugar
8 to 12 ounces bow-tie pasta (farfalle)
$1/4$ cup chopped fresh parsley
2 ounces crumbled feta cheese or grated Parmesan cheese
8 to 12 basil leaves (optional garnish)

Helpful Hint:

Although ripe tomatoes and fresh basil are hard to find in the middle of winter, they are worth the hunt for this special occasion.

In a medium saucepan, heat the oil over medium-high heat. Add the garlic, zucchini, and all the mushrooms and cook, stirring, for 5 to 7 minutes.

Add the tomatoes, oregano, basil, salt, pepper, and sugar, and cook for about 10 to 15 minutes over medium-low heat, stirring frequently. Set aside for 10 minutes before serving.

Meanwhile, cook the pasta according to package directions until al dente, about 9 to 12 minutes. Drain, and transfer the pasta to a large serving bowl and cover until ready to serve.

To serve, spoon the sauce over the pasta and sprinkle the parsley and cheese over the top. Garnish the edge of the plates with basil leaves if desired.

Makes *2* servings

Per Serving: 464 Calories; 15g Protein; 13g Fat; 67g Carbohydrates; 25mg Cholesterol; 882mg Sodium; 8g Fiber.

Chocolate-Dipped Strawberries Coated with Hazelnuts

¹/₂ cup semisweet chocolate chips
2 tablespoons coffee liqueur or Irish cream liqueur
10 to 12 large strawberries, rinsed and patted dry
¹/₂ cup finely chopped hazelnuts

Combine the chocolate chips and liqueur in a small bowl. Microwave the mixture until melted, about 30 seconds. Alternatively, combine the chocolate chips and liqueur in the top of a double boiler and cook over medium heat, stirring frequently, until fully melted, about 5 minutes.

Dip the tips of the strawberries into the melted chocolate mixture and then roll the fruit in the nuts. Place the fruit with the stem side down on a plate and chill until serving time.

Makes 2 servings

Per Serving (5 strawberries): 547 Calories; 6g Protein; 37g Fat; 45g Carbohydrates; 0mg Cholesterol; 3mg Sodium; 4g Fiber.

a Chinese  Banquet

Vegetable Dumplings • Hoisin Dipping Sauce • Sesame Scallion Pancakes •

Asian Vegetable and Tofu Stir-Fry • Five-Spice Rice • Yard-Long Beans

with Crispy Almonds • Sweet Adzuki Bean Soup

makes *6* servings

Asian Vegetable and Tofu Stir-Fry (page 24) (served with Five-Spice Rice, page 24)
and Sweet Adzuki Bean Soup (page 25)

*T*he Chinese New Year, which falls between January 21 and February 19, is buoyed by optimism, renewal, and elaborate traditions. It is Christmas Day, New Year's Eve, and Thanksgiving all wrapped into one. Symbols abound: Dried watermelon seeds augur good fortune, the green hue of vegetables symbolizes youth, dates represent abundance, and the seeds in pomegranates predict many children. Firecrackers are lit to frighten away evil spirits.

With hope and thoughts of prosperity in the air, the Chinese New Year festivity centers on a sumptuous feast. This vegetarian menu reflects the kinds of food served throughout the holiday. The meal beckons with the intense and ethereal flavors of the Orient—ginger, sesame oil, hoisin and soy sauce, and Chinese five-spice powder, a fragrant blend of star anise, cloves, cinnamon, Szechuan pepper, and fennel.

The banquet includes delicate Vegetable Dumplings filled with shredded Chinese cabbage, carrots, and Asian spices. The dumplings are enhanced with a few drops of a pungent-sweet Hoisin Dipping Sauce. This New Year's meal also features Sesame Scallion Pancakes, thin crepes with simple but enticing flavors.

A stir-fry, of course, commands center stage. This menu revolves around the Asian Vegetable and Tofu Stir-Fry, a pleasing combination of eggplant, bell peppers, tofu, and sprouts, coated with a velvety red sauce. Five-Spice Rice complements the stir-fry while soaking up a pool of flavors.

Rounding out the table is a platter of Yard-Long Beans with Crispy Almonds. Yard-long beans, also called Chinese long beans, are pencil-thin, mild-tasting beans, similar to green beans. The fresh beans are deftly seasoned with garlic, almonds, and a hint of soy sauce. When all of these dishes are served together, a grand culinary mosaic of Asian flavors takes shape.

The Chinese don't eat dessert at the end of a meal in the Western fashion. Sweets are traditionally eaten as snacks or between meals. However, this vegetarian banquet is lighter than most and leaves room for dessert; besides, it's a New Year's celebration. This menu's finale is Sweet Adzuki Bean Soup (also known as sweet red bean paste soup or *shiruko*), a piping hot, tantalizing Chinese specialty savored on special occasions. Red adzuki beans, also called aduki beans, are often used in Chinese pastries and sweet breads and impart a nutty flavor and chewy texture for this most interesting and surprising finish.

Although this meal was designed with the Chinese New Year in mind, you can serve it any time. It is perfect when you are in the mood to experience the lighter, more healthful side of Chinese cuisine.

Kitchen Countdown

2 days before	Soak the adzuki beans overnight.
1 day before	Make the Sweet Adzuki Bean Soup; cool to room temperature, cover, and refrigerate. Make the Hoisin Dipping Sauce while the beans cook; cover and refrigerate.
3 to 4 hours before	Cut up the stir-fry vegetables, cover or wrap, and refrigerate.
2 to 2½ hours before	Make the Vegetable Dumplings. Cover and keep warm in 200° F oven.
1½ hours before	Make the Sesame Scallion Pancakes. Cover and keep warm in a 200° F oven.
30 minutes before	Make the Asian Vegetable and Tofu Stir-Fry. Cook the Five-Spice Rice.
15 minutes before	Stir-fry the Yard-Long Beans with Crispy Almonds. Reheat the Sweet Adzuki Bean Soup over low heat and keep warm throughout the dinner.
Dinnertime	Start with tea. Serve all of the dishes at the table family style, reserving the sweet bean soup for dessert. Encourage the guests to spoon the Hoisin Dipping Sauce over the Vegetable Dumplings and Sesame Scallion Pancakes. Keep plenty of hot tea at the ready during the meal.
What guests can bring	Everyone can bring a favorite Chinese tea, such as Darjeeling, orange pekoe, oolong, or green tea, or a holiday pastry from a local Chinese grocery store.

Vegetable Dumplings

4 cups finely chopped Chinese or napa
    cabbage
$^{1}/_{2}$ teaspoon salt
1 tablespoon rice wine or dry sherry
1 tablespoon low-sodium or regular
    soy sauce
2 teaspoons cornstarch
1 teaspoon sesame oil

1 tablespoon canola or peanut oil
12 to 14 button mushrooms, chopped
1 tablespoon minced fresh gingerroot
1 cup shredded carrots
30 to 36 round dumpling or wonton
    wrappers
Hoisin Dipping Sauce (recipe follows)

Helpful Hint:

Chinese and napa cabbage
are light green head lettuces
with tightly furled, crinkly
leaves. The cabbage, along
with dumpling wrappers,
sesame oil, and rice wine,
can be found in Asian grocery
stores and well-stocked
supermarkets.

Place the cabbage in a colander and sprinkle with the salt. Let stand
for 30 minutes. Drain and squeeze out the excess liquid. Set aside.

In a small mixing bowl, mix together the rice wine or sherry, soy
sauce, cornstarch, and sesame oil. Set aside.

In a large nonstick skillet or wok, heat the canola or peanut oil over
medium heat. Add the mushrooms and ginger and stir-fry for about
7 minutes. Add the cabbage and carrots and stir-fry for 1 minute more.
Stir in the soy sauce mixture and stir-fry for 1 minute more. Remove
from the heat and let cool for about 15 minutes.

Place a round dumpling wrapper on the work surface. Spoon about
1 heaping teaspoon of the filling in the center of a dumpling wrapper.
Moisten the edges of the dumpling with a little water and fold the wrapper over to form a half-moon shape. Pinch the edges together to form
a seal. Place the filled dumpling on a flat tray. Continue filling the
remaining dumpling wrappers and arrange on the tray.

Meanwhile, in a large pot or saucepan, bring $2^{1}/_{2}$ to 3 quarts of water
to a boil. Gently drop in half of the dumplings and return to a boil. Cook
over medium heat, stirring occasionally, until the dumplings puff up
slightly, about 5 to 7 minutes. Carefully remove the dumplings with a
large slotted spoon and place on a serving platter. Cover the finished
dumplings until ready to serve. Continue cooking the remaining
dumplings in the same manner and place on the platter.

Serve the dumplings with Hoisin Dipping Sauce (recipe follows).

Makes about 30 dumplings, 5 dumplings per serving

Per Serving of 5 Dumplings: 238 Calories; 10g Protein; 3g Fat; 43g Carbohydrates;
0mg Cholesterol; 273mg Sodium; 3g Fiber.

Hoisin Dipping Sauce

¼ cup hoisin sauce
3 to 4 tablespoons low-sodium or regular soy sauce
2 tablespoons water
1 scallion, chopped
1 teaspoon rice vinegar

Helpful Hint:

Hoisin sauce is a sweet-and-spicy, dark brown sauce with the consistency of molasses. Hoisin sauce and rice vinegar can be found in Asian grocery stores and well-stocked supermarkets.

In a small mixing bowl, combine all of the ingredients. Cover and refrigerate until ready to serve with the dumplings. Makes about ½ cup.

Per Tablespoon: 7 Calories; 0.7g Protein; 0 Fat; 1g Carbohydrate; 0mg Cholesterol; 267mg Sodium; 0.1g Fiber.

Sesame Scallion Pancakes

2 cups unbleached white flour or cake flour
1 teaspoon salt
1 large egg plus 1 large egg white, beaten
1½ cups water
2 teaspoons sesame oil
4 large whole scallions, trimmed and finely chopped
1 tablespoon canola or peanut oil, approximately

In a medium mixing bowl, combine the flour and salt. Blend in the egg, egg white, water, and sesame oil and mix until the batter is smooth. Fold in the scallions.

Heat about 1 teaspoon of the canola or peanut oil in an 8-inch, non-stick skillet over medium heat. Ladle about ¼ cup of batter into the skillet and spread it out to form a thin pancake about 8 inches in diameter. Cook for 2 to 3 minutes until the edges are lightly brown. Flip the pancake and cook for 1 to 2 minutes more until the bottom is light brown. Transfer the pancake to a warm plate and cover with waxed paper.

Continue making pancakes with the remaining batter. Add a little oil to the skillet after every other pancake. To serve, roll up like an unfilled crepe.

Makes *10* pancakes

Per Pancake: 110 Calories; 3g Protein; 3g Fat; 17g Carbohydrates; 27mg Cholesterol; 226mg Sodium; 0.9g Fiber.

Asian Vegetable and Tofu Stir-Fry

1 tablespoon canola or peanut oil
2 medium Japanese eggplants or
 1 medium Italian eggplant,
 halved and julienned
2 red or yellow bell peppers, julienned
1/2 pound extra firm tofu, julienned
8 ounces sliced water chestnuts, drained
1/2 pound fresh snow peas, tips removed

1 tablespoon minced fresh gingerroot
1 jalapeño or other chile pepper, seeded
 and minced (optional)
6 tablespoons low-sodium or regular
 soy sauce
2 teaspoons sesame oil
One 15-ounce can tomato sauce
2 ounces mung bean sprouts

In a large wok or nonstick skillet, heat the oil over medium-high heat. Add the eggplants and bell peppers and stir-fry for 6 to 7 minutes. Add the tofu, water chestnuts, snow peas, ginger, and jalapeño, if desired, and stir-fry for 1 to 2 minutes more. Stir in the soy sauce and sesame oil and stir-fry for 2 minutes more.

Reduce the heat to low and stir in the tomato sauce and sprouts. Simmer for 5 to 7 minutes, stirring frequently. Transfer the vegetables and sauce to a serving platter, cover, and keep warm until ready to serve. Offer the Five-Spice Rice (recipe follows) on the side.

Makes 6 servings

Per Serving: 130 Calories; 8g Protein; 5g Fat; 13g Carbohydrates; 0mg Cholesterol; 628mg Sodium; 6g Fiber.

Five-Spice Rice

2 cups basmati or other long-grain white rice
4 cups water
1 teaspoon five-spice powder
1/2 teaspoon salt
3 or 4 whole scallions, trimmed and chopped

In a large saucepan, combine the rice, water, five-spice powder, and salt, and bring to a boil. Cover the pan, reduce the heat to low, and cook until all of the liquid is absorbed, about 15 to 20 minutes.

Remove from the heat, fluff the rice with a fork, and fold in the scallions. Let stand covered for at least 10 minutes before serving. Offer as a side dish to Asian Vegetable and Tofu Stir-Fry (previous recipe).

Makes 6 servings

Per Serving: 170 Calories; 3g Protein; 0.2g Fat; 38g Carbohydrates; 0mg Cholesterol; 135mg Sodium; 0.9g Fiber.

Yard-Long Beans with Crispy Almonds

2 teaspoons peanut oil
1½ to 2 pounds yard-long beans, trimmed and cut into 2- to 3-inch pieces
2 or 3 cloves garlic, minced
1 cup slivered almonds
¼ cup low-sodium or regular soy sauce
2 teaspoons brown sugar

Helpful Hint:

Yard-long beans can be found in Asian grocery stores and well-stocked supermarkets. Fresh green beans may be substituted.

In a large skillet or wok, heat the oil over medium-high heat. Add the beans and stir-fry for about 5 minutes. Stir in the garlic and almonds and stir-fry for 2 minutes more. Stir in the soy sauce and brown sugar and stir-fry for 1 minute more.

Cover the beans and keep warm until ready to serve. Serve the beans on a large oval platter.

Makes *6* servings

Per Serving: 168 Calories; 5g Protein; 12g Fat; 9g Carbohydrates; 0mg Cholesterol; 405mg Sodium; 4g Fiber.

Sweet Adzuki Bean Soup

1 cup dry adzuki beans
4 cups water
1 cup plus 2 tablespoons brown sugar

Helpful Hint:

Adzuki beans, also called aduki beans, are small pea-shaped beans with a dark burgundy hue and tiny white eye. They can be found in most Asian grocery stores, natural food stores, and well-stocked supermarkets.

Soak the beans in plenty of water to cover for at least 4 hours, preferably overnight; drain.

In a medium saucepan, combine the beans and 4 cups fresh water and bring to a simmer. Cook, uncovered, over medium-low heat, stirring occasionally, until the beans are tender, about 1½ hours.

Stir in the sugar and cook for 5 to 7 minutes more over low heat, stirring frequently. Remove from the heat and let cool slightly. Serve the soup in small soup bowls or refrigerate for later.

To reheat, bring to a simmer over medium heat before serving.

Makes *8* servings

Per Serving: 313 Calories; 10g Protein; 1g Fat; 66g Carbohydrates; 0mg Cholesterol; 27mg Sodium; 6g Fiber.

a
Brazilian
Weekend
Afternoon

Hearts of Palm Vinaigrette • Feijoada (Black Bean Stew) • Yellow Rice •

Lemon-Braised Kale • Coconut Tapioca Pudding

recipes make *6* servings

Feijoada (Black Bean Stew, page 30) and Yellow Rice (page 31)

Brazil is famous for wild carnivals, exotic beaches, samba music, and a lavish feast called *feijoada completa* (literally, a "complete dish of beans"). From bustling Rio de Janeiro to the countryside villages, Brazilians enjoy this copious and nourishing midday meal usually on the weekend. The dishes are presented in large serving bowls at the table and are served family style. Guests help themselves. (It is said that no one should go to work after indulging in such a hearty spread.)

This healthful version retains the spirit and authentic flavors of the Brazilian tradition *sans* meat. The meal begins with Hearts of Palm Vinaigrette, a salad of hearts of palm, a delicacy reminiscent of marinated artichoke hearts. This initial nibbling gives way to the Feijoada, or Black Bean Stew, a cauldron of smoldering black beans, chunky vegetables, and earthy herbs. (*Feijão* is Portuguese for "beans.")

Lemon-Braised Kale (or you could substitute spinach) and aromatic Yellow Rice accompany the Feijoada. A hot sauce or salsa is also welcome. (Try Habanero Salsa, page 96, but substitute a jalapeño for the habanero pepper.)

Brazilians love coconut treats, so for dessert, there is Coconut Tapioca Pudding. (The Brazilian name is *cuscus*, pronounced like "couscous," but not to be confused with the tiny semolina grain.) The pudding has a thick, gelatinous texture and is sliced like a pie. For a distinctly decadent spin, spoon a little chocolate sauce or hot fudge over the top.

This is the perfect menu to serve around the time of the Brazilian carnival, an annual spring extravaganza similar to Mardi Gras. It also makes an unpretentious and filling dinner for friends and family who have not yet indulged in the gustatory pleasures of *feijoada completa*.

Kitchen Countdown

1 day before	Soak the black beans for the Feijoada in plenty of water. Make the Coconut Tapioca Pudding. Cool to room temperature, cover, and refrigerate.
2¹/₂ hours before	Drain the beans, discarding the soaking liquid. Cook the beans in fresh water. While the beans simmer, make the Hearts of Palm Vinaigrette and refrigerate.
1¹/₂ hours before	Finish preparing the Feijoada.
30 minutes before	Make the Yellow Rice and Lemon-Braised Kale.
Dinnertime	Present the dishes in large serving platters at the table and serve family style, saving the Coconut Tapioca Pudding for last, of course. Fill the air with samba music or merengue music and set the table with brightly colored fabrics.
What guests can bring	This meal calls out for strong, dark beer, the kind brewed at microbreweries.

Hearts of Palm Vinaigrette

5 tablespoons olive oil
2$\frac{1}{2}$ tablespoons red wine vinegar
2 tablespoons chopped fresh parsley
$\frac{1}{4}$ teaspoon salt
$\frac{1}{4}$ teaspoon freshly ground black pepper

Two or three 14-ounce cans hearts of
    palm, drained, rinsed and sliced
    crosswise into $\frac{1}{2}$-inch sections
3 large tomatoes, diced
1 medium red onion, chopped
1 small head romaine or red leaf lettuce

Helpful Hint:

Hearts of palm can be found
in the canned food sections
of supermarkets.

In a large mixing bowl, combine the oil, vinegar, parsley, salt, and pepper.
Gently mix in the hearts of palm, tomatoes, and onion.

Refrigerate for at least 2 hours before serving. Serve over a bed of
romaine leaves or red leaf lettuce.

Makes 6 servings

*Per Serving: 132 Calories; 5g Protein; 5g Fat; 21g Carbohydrates; 0mg Cholesterol;
178mg Sodium; 9g Fiber.*

Feijoada (Black Bean Stew)

2 cups dried black beans, soaked
    overnight and drained
10 cups water
1 tablespoon canola oil
1 large yellow onion, diced
2 green or red bell peppers, diced
2 medium tomatoes, diced
4 cloves garlic, minced

3 to 4 medium red potatoes, coarsely
    chopped
4 medium carrots, peeled and coarsely
    chopped
2 teaspoons dried thyme leaves
1$\frac{1}{2}$ teaspoons ground cumin
1 teaspoon salt
1 teaspoon freshly ground black pepper
$\frac{1}{2}$ cup chopped fresh parsley

In a large saucepan, combine the beans and water. Cook over low heat
until the beans are tender, about 1 to 1$\frac{1}{2}$ hours; drain, reserving 3$\frac{1}{2}$ cups
of the cooking liquid. Heat the oil over medium heat in a large saucepan
and add the onion, bell peppers, tomatoes, and garlic. Cook, stirring, for
8 to 10 minutes. Add the beans, reserved cooking liquid, potatoes, carrots,
thyme, cumin, salt, and pepper, and cook, uncovered, over medium-low
heat, stirring occasionally, for 50 minutes to 1 hour. Stir in the parsley.
Let stand for 10 to 15 minutes before serving.

Ladle into a large serving bowl or cauldron and serve with Yellow Rice
and Lemon-Braised Kale.

Makes 6 servings

*Per Serving: 333 Calories; 16g Protein; 4g Fat; 62g Carbohydrates; 0mg Cholesterol;
386mg Sodium; 17g Fiber.*

Yellow Rice

2¹/₂ cups white basmati rice or jasmine rice
5 cups hot water
¹/₂ teaspoon salt
¹/₂ teaspoon ground white pepper
¹/₃ teaspoon ground turmeric

In a large saucepan, combine all ingredients and bring to a boil. Cover the pan, reduce the heat to low, and cook until all of the liquid is absorbed, about 15 to 20 minutes.

Remove from the heat and fluff the rice with a fork. Let stand (covered) for at least 10 minutes before serving.

Makes 6 servings

Per Serving: 185 Calories; 4g Protein; 0g Fat; 41g Carbohydrates; 0mg Cholesterol; 180mg Sodium; 0.9g Fiber.

Lemon-Braised Kale

2 medium bunches kale (about 2 lbs.) or two 10-ounce bags fresh spinach
2 tablespoons olive oil
1 large red onion, chopped
2 or 3 cloves garlic, minced
Juice of 2 large lemons
¹/₂ teaspoon salt
¹/₂ teaspoon freshly ground black pepper

Rinse the kale or spinach in a colander under cold running water. Cut off the stems and coarsely chop the leaves. Set aside.

In a large saucepan, heat the oil over medium-high heat. Add the onion and garlic and cook, stirring, for 3 to 4 minutes. Add the kale or spinach, lemon juice, salt, and pepper, and cook over medium-low heat until the greens are wilted, about 4 to 6 minutes. Transfer to a shallow serving platter and keep warm until ready to serve.

Makes 6 servings

Per Serving: 135 Calories; 5g Protein; 6g Fat; 20g Carbohydrates; 0mg Cholesterol; 243mg Sodium; 4g Fiber.

Coconut Tapioca Pudding

1¹/₄ cups granulated tapioca
1 cup shredded coconut, preferably unsweetened
2¹/₂ cups 1% or 2% milk
¹/₂ cup sugar
¹/₄ cup low-fat, sweetened, condensed milk or
    1 cup semisweet chocolate chips, melted (optional)

Combine the tapioca, coconut, milk, and sugar in a medium saucepan. Bring to a simmer over high heat, stirring frequently. Reduce the heat to low and cook, stirring constantly, for 3 minutes more.

Transfer the pudding to an 8-inch square baking pan and let cool to room temperature. Cover and refrigerate for 3 to 4 hours (preferably overnight) before serving. The pudding will become quite firm.

If you are in a decadent mood, pour the condensed milk over the top of the pudding before serving. Or melt semisweet chocolate chips in the microwave and spread over the top. To serve, slice the pudding into squares.

Makes 6 servings

Per Serving: 273 Calories; 4g Protein; 5g Fat; 55g Carbohydrates; 4mg Cholesterol; 83mg Sodium; 0.8g Fiber.

a Jazzy *Taste of* New Orleans

Gumbo Z' Herbes • Wild Pecan Rice • Cracked Pepper Cornbread •

Quinoa-Vegetable Jambalaya • Red Hot Red Beans and Broccoli •

Banana-Strawberry Flambé

recipes make *4* servings

Quinoa-Vegetable Jambalaya (page 39), Red Hot Red Beans and Broccoli (page 40),
and Cracked Pepper Cornbread (page 39)

Creole and Cajun cooking, the renowned fare of the Louisiana territory, is bold, boisterous, and bebopping with flavor. The food is down-to-earth and unpretentious, yet vibrant and festive. Creole and Cajun meals are celebrations of eating and indulging, and when it comes to spicing, to heck with moderation.

In Louisiana kitchens, green peppers, onions, and celery are used so often that they are referred to as the "holy trinity." A trio of ground peppers—black, white, and cayenne—give Cajun and Creole cooking an assertive yet well-rounded spiciness. Fresh and dried herbs—oregano, parsley, and thyme—add depth and dimension.

This menu is a classic New Orleans feast that can be served anytime, but Mardi Gras is perfect. The meal begins with Gumbo Z' Herbes, a piquant soup populated with a variety of leafy greens. Legend has it that you will make a new friend for every kind of green you add to the soup. Gumbo is traditionally served over rice, in this case Wild Pecan Rice, a grain grown in Louisiana. Wild Pecan Rice is neither wild nor does it contain pecans, but it does have an aromatic scent reminiscent of wild rice, popcorn, and pecans. It is similar to Indian basmati rice.

For the main dish, there is Quinoa-Vegetable Jambalaya, a meal as fun as its name. This meatless rendition features a cornucopia of vegetables and spices and is made, of course, with quinoa, a protein-rich grain, in place of rice. Jambalaya is accompanied by the classic side dish of robust red kidney beans. For this healthful version, which we call Red Hot Red Beans and Broccoli, crunchy broccoli replaces chunks of overcooked meat, so there is a net gain in both flavor and nutrients. A moist Cracked Pepper Cornbread is passed at the table.

This high-impact meal needs a light, low-impact dessert with a touch of flamboyance. Thus, Banana-Strawberry Flambé, also called Bananas Foster in New Orleans, will light up your guests' eyes as well as their taste buds.

Kitchen Countdown

1 day before	Prepare the Gumbo Z' Herbes; cool to room temperature, cover, and refrigerate.
4 hours before	Make the Cracked Pepper Cornbread.
1½ hours before	Start the Quinoa-Vegetable Jambalaya.
1 hour before	Make the Red Hot Red Beans and Broccoli.
30 minutes before	Make the Wild Pecan Rice; reheat the gumbo.
Dinnertime	For a Mardi Gras theme, set the tables with masks and pull out the sparklers and horns left over from July 4th and New Year's Eve. A fruit punch spiked with rum will put the guests in the proper Bourbon Street frame of mind.
	For the meal, serve the gumbo with the rice, followed by the jambalaya, cornbread, and red beans and broccoli. After dinner, prepare the fruit flambé.
What guests can bring	Low-fat frozen yogurt for the flambé. Compact discs to put guests in a New Orleans mood: Louis Armstrong, Benny Goodman, Sarah Vaughan, Ella Fitzgerald, Billie Holiday, Dr. John, Buckwheat Zydeco.

Gumbo Z' Herbes

1 tablespoon canola oil
1 medium yellow onion, diced
1 green or red bell pepper, seeded and
    diced
1 stalk celery, chopped
2 or 3 cloves garlic, minced
6 cups vegetable stock or water
One 14-ounce can stewed tomatoes
1 cup chopped okra (fresh or frozen)
1/4 cup tomato paste
1 1/2 teaspoons dried oregano

1 teaspoon dried thyme
1/2 teaspoon freshly ground black pepper
1/4 teaspoon cayenne pepper
1 teaspoon salt
4 cups chopped mixed greens, such as
    spinach, mustard greens, kale, or
    dandelion greens (remember, a friend
    gained for each kind added)
2 to 3 tablespoons chopped fresh parsley
4 cups cooked Wild Pecan Rice (recipe
    follows) or basmati rice

Helpful Hint:

Wild Pecan Rice, which looks like pale yellow basmati rice and is a Cajun favorite, is available in well-stocked supermarkets.

In a large saucepan, heat the oil over medium-high heat. Add the onion, bell pepper, celery, and garlic and cook, stirring, until the vegetables are tender, about 5 to 7 minutes. Stir in the vegetable stock or water, stewed tomatoes, okra, tomato paste, oregano, thyme, black pepper, cayenne, and salt, and bring to a simmer. Lower the heat to medium-low and cook for 15 minutes, stirring occasionally.

Stir in the mixed greens and cook for about 15 minutes more. Stir in the parsley and remove from the heat.

When ready to serve, place about 1/2 cup cooked Wild Pecan Rice in the bottom of each soup bowl. Ladle the gumbo over the rice.

Makes 4 servings

Per Serving with 1/2 cup Wild Pecan Rice: 284 Calories; 8g Protein; 4g Fat; 57g Carbohydrates; 0mg Cholesterol; 1,148mg Sodium; 7g Fiber.

Wild Pecan Rice

1 1/4 cups wild pecan rice or basmati rice
2 cups water
1/2 teaspoon salt
1/4 teaspoon white pepper

In a medium saucepan, combine all ingredients. Bring to a simmer over medium-high heat and cover. Cook for 15 to 20 minutes over low heat (do not stir). Remove from the heat and fluff the rice with a fork. Cover and set aside for 10 minutes before serving.

Cracked Pepper Cornbread

1 cup yellow cornmeal
1 cup unbleached white flour
1/3 cup sugar
1 tablespoon baking powder
1/2 teaspoon salt
1/2 tablespoon whole black peppercorns,
    coarsely crushed

1 large egg plus 1 egg white, beaten
1 cup buttermilk, 1% milk, or soy milk
1/4 cup canola oil
2 tablespoons chopped pimientos or
    roasted red bell peppers
1 cup corn kernels, fresh or frozen and
    thawed

Preheat the oven to 375° F. Combine the cornmeal, flour, sugar, baking powder, salt, and peppercorns in a mixing bowl and blend together.

In a separate bowl, whisk together the egg and egg white, buttermilk, milk, or soy milk, oil, and pimientos or roasted peppers. Stir in the corn.

Gently fold the liquid ingredients into the dry ingredients until the mixture forms a batter. Pour the batter into a greased 9-inch round deep-dish baking pan or springform pan. Bake on the middle rack until the crust is lightly browned and a toothpick inserted in the center comes out clean, about 20 to 25 minutes. Remove from the heat and let cool on a rack.

Cut into pie-shaped wedges and serve with Quinoa-Vegetable Jambalaya (recipe follows).

Makes *6* servings

Per Serving: 319 Calories; 8g Protein; 11g Fat; 49g Carbohydrates; 37mg Cholesterol; 493mg Sodium; 3g Fiber.

Quinoa-Vegetable Jambalaya

1 1/4 cups quinoa, rinsed and drained
2 1/2 cups hot water
1 tablespoon canola oil
1 green bell pepper, seeded and diced
1 medium yellow onion, diced
1 medium zucchini, halved and sliced
    diagonally into 1/2-inch slices
2 cups diced eggplant, unpeeled (about
    1 small eggplant)
12 to 14 button mushrooms, sliced
1 celery stalk, sliced

2 to 3 cloves garlic, minced
One 28-ounce can crushed tomatoes
1/4 cup water
1 1/2 tablespoons dried parsley
    (3 tablespoons chopped fresh)
2 teaspoons dried oregano
1 teaspoon dried thyme
1/2 teaspoon salt
1/2 teaspoon freshly ground black pepper
Hot pepper sauce to taste

Combine the quinoa and water in a medium saucepan. Bring to a simmer and cover. Cook over low heat until all of the water is absorbed, about 15 to 20 minutes. Set aside.

(continues)

In a large saucepan, heat the oil. Add the green pepper, onion, zucchini, eggplant, mushrooms, celery, and garlic. Cook over medium heat for 8 to 10 minutes, stirring frequently. Stir in remaining ingredients except quinoa, and cook over low heat for 15 to 20 minutes, stirring occasionally.

When ready to serve, fold in the cooked quinoa and cook for 5 minutes more over low heat, stirring frequently. Serve with Red Hot Red Beans and Broccoli (recipe follows) on the side. Pass the hot pepper sauce at the table.

Makes 4 **servings**

Per Serving: 350 Calories; 15g Protein; 7g Fat; 62g Carbohydrates; 0mg Cholesterol; 1,092mg Sodium; 11g Fiber.

Red Hot Red Beans and Broccoli

1 tablespoon canola oil
1 medium yellow onion, diced
1 red bell pepper, seeded and diced
1 stalk celery, chopped
Two 15-ounce cans red kidney beans, drained
One 14-ounce can stewed tomatoes
1 medium bunch broccoli (about 1¹/₂ pounds), cut into florets

¹/₂ cup water
1 to 2 teaspoons hot pepper sauce
¹/₂ teaspoon freshly ground black pepper
¹/₂ teaspoon salt
¹/₄ teaspoon cayenne pepper
2 to 3 tablespoons chopped fresh parsley

In a large saucepan, heat the oil over medium-high heat. Add the onion, bell pepper, and celery and cook, stirring, for 5 to 7 minutes.

Stir in all remaining ingredients except parsley; cover and cook, stirring occasionally, over medium-low heat until the broccoli is tender, about 12 to 15 minutes.

Stir in the parsley and remove from the heat. Set aside for at least 15 minutes. Serve on the side of the Quinoa-Vegetable Jambalaya (previous recipe).

Makes 4 **servings**

Per Serving: 298 Calories; 16g Protein; 4g Fat; 51g Carbohydrates; 0mg Cholesterol; 1,369mg Sodium; 20g Fiber.

Banana-Strawberry Flambé

¼ cup apple juice
2 tablespoons brown sugar
4 bananas, peeled and sliced crosswise
½ pint strawberries, rinsed and sliced
¼ teaspoon ground cinnamon or allspice
¼ cup dark rum
Splash of banana liqueur (optional)
2 pints low-fat vanilla frozen yogurt

Combine the apple juice and brown sugar in a skillet and cook over medium heat for about 3 minutes, stirring frequently.

Add the bananas, strawberries, and cinnamon or allspice, and cook for 3 to 4 minutes more, gently turning the fruit every minute or so as it cooks, coating it with the juice mixture. Remove the pan from the heat and add the rum and liqueur, if desired. Return to medium heat and bring to a simmer. Carefully touch a lighted match to the pan, flambéing the fruit. Allow the flame to subside and continue cooking for 1 minute more. Scoop the frozen yogurt into small dessert bowls and spoon the fruit over the top.

Makes *4* servings

Helpful Hint:

When flambéing, never pour liquor directly from the bottle to the pan. Always measure out the liquor and transfer it to a small pitcher ahead of time. Then pour liquid from pitcher.

Per Serving: 393 Calories; 9g Protein; 5g Fat; 78g Carbohydrates; 14mg Cholesterol; 104mg Sodium; 4g Fiber.

Passover *Seder*

Apple-Date Haroset • Matzo Ball and Vegetable Soup •

Roasted Beets with Horseradish-Watercress Vinaigrette • Spinach-Potato Kugel •

Lemon-Dressed Asparagus • Coco-Nut Macaroons

recipes make *6* to *8* servings

Matzo Ball and Vegetable Soup (page 46) and Apple-Date Haroset (page 46)

To the Jewish faithful, Passover is a time for reflection and remembrance. Passover revolves around the Seder, a sacred dinner ritual. Family and friends read from the Haggadah, a Passover prayer book recounting the exodus of the Jewish people from Egypt. The night is filled with joyous, thoughtful, and solemn moments.

The menu is replete with symbolism. Only unleavened bread made from matzo meal can be eaten; as Jews fled Egypt, they did not have time to wait for the bread to rise. Haroset, a chunky fruit-and-nut condiment, signifies the mortar used by Jewish ancestors to build the pyramids of Egypt. A bitter herb (such as horseradish) represents the bitter tears shed by the enslaved Jews.

Green sprigs of parsley signify the renewal and optimism that comes with spring. The roundness of a boiled egg symbolizes the circle of life and death. Traditionally, a shank bone has been used to symbolize the lamb sacrificed to God; vegetarians will substitute a roasted beet.

With a little ingenuity, it is easy to a create a meatless Seder. This particular menu also is suitable for advance preparation, which of course makes life easier for the host. The Matzo Ball and Vegetable Soup is prepared with an aromatic vegetable broth and made a day ahead to give the flavors ample time to meld. The sweet and savory Apple-Date Haroset can also be made well in advance. (But be careful; it is tempting to eat it by the spoonful.) Roasted Beets, enhanced with Horseradish-Watercress Vinaigrette, also benefit from advance preparation.

The Spinach-Potato Kugel, a hearty casserole dish, replaces the typical meat main dish. The side dish of Lemon-Dressed Asparagus is lightly coated with a tangy lemon dressing. The dessert is a tray of flourless "Coco-Nut" Macaroon cookies, chewy morsels made with coconut, almonds, and cocoa. These too can be made one or two days ahead of time.

Kitchen Countdown

1 day before	Make the Coco-Nut Macaroons. Store in an airtight container. Make Matzo Ball and Vegetable Soup, but refrigerate the matzo balls and soup separately. Prepare Roasted Beets with Horseradish-Watercress Vinaigrette; cover and refrigerate.
3 to 4 hours or 1 day before	Make the Apple-Date Haroset; cover and refrigerate.
1½ hours before	Make the Spinach-Potato Kugel.
½ hour before	Bring the vegetable soup to a simmer; add the matzo balls and cook for about 15 minutes over low heat. Keep hot until ready to serve. Transfer Roasted Beets with Horseradish-Watercress Vinaigrette to a serving platter.
Just minutes before	Prepare the Lemon-Dressed Asparagus.
Dinnertime	After (or during) the reading from the Haggadah, serve the Matzo Ball and Vegetable Soup. After the soup, the rest of the food can be served either one dish at a time or family style. If served in courses, pass the Apple-Date Haroset with the matzo crackers, followed by the Roasted Beets with Horseradish-Watercress Vinaigrette. The next course should include both the Spinach-Potato Kugel and the Lemon-Dressed Asparagus. The Coco-Nut Macaroons are passed at the table after the meal.
What guests can bring	Passover wine. A bouquet of spring flowers.

Apple-Date Haroset

2 red apples, diced (peeled if desired)
1 cup chopped, pitted dates
1 cup chopped walnuts
$^1/_2$ cup dark raisins

$^1/_4$ cup sweet Passover wine
1 tablespoon honey
$^1/_8$ teaspoon cinnamon

Combine all of the ingredients in a mixing bowl and blend well. Refrigerate until ready to serve. Stir the haroset before serving.

Makes about *8* **half-cup servings**

Per $^1/_2$ Cup: 203 Calories; 3g Protein; 9g Fat; 30g Carbohydrates; 0mg Cholesterol; 6mg Sodium; 3g Fiber.

Matzo Ball and Vegetable Soup

$1^1/_2$ tablespoons canola oil
1 medium yellow onion, chopped
2 cups chopped leeks (rinsed thoroughly)
2 stalks celery, diced
1 red bell pepper, seeded and diced
2 cloves garlic, minced
8 cups hot water or vegetable stock
4 medium carrots, peeled and diced

1 teaspoon salt
$^1/_2$ teaspoon freshly ground black pepper
$^1/_3$ pound green beans, cut into 2-inch
sections
$^1/_4$ cup chopped fresh parsley
12 cooked Matzo Balls, approximately
(recipe follows)

Heat the oil in a large saucepan or soup pot over medium heat. Add the onion, leeks, celery, bell pepper, and garlic and cook, stirring, for 5 to 7 minutes. Stir in the water or stock, carrots, salt, and pepper, and bring to a boil. Cook over medium-low heat for 20 minutes, stirring occasionally.

Add the green beans and parsley and cook for 5 minutes more over low heat. Remove from the heat and cool to room temperature. Refrigerate for 4 hours or overnight.

Prepare the Matzo Balls.

When ready to serve, pour the soup into a saucepan or soup pot and bring to a simmer. Add the cooked matzo balls and cook for 10 to 15 minutes over low heat. To serve, place a matzo ball in each soup bowl and ladle the soup over the top.

Makes *6* **servings**

Per Serving: 172 Calories; 5g Protein; 9g Fat; 21g Carbohydrates; 41mg Cholesterol; 409mg Sodium; 5g Fiber.

Matzo Balls

3 large eggs
3 tablespoons canola oil
¹/₄ cup matzo meal
1 teaspoon salt (optional)
3 tablespoons water

In a mixing bowl, beat the eggs. Add the oil and beat again. Fold in the matzo meal and salt if desired. Blend in the water. Cover the dough and refrigerate for about 15 minutes.

In a large saucepan or Dutch oven, bring about 2 quarts of water to a boil. Remove the matzo dough from the refrigerator. With moist hands, form the dough into small balls about the size of golf balls, and drop into the boiling water. Cover the pan and simmer over medium-low heat for about 30 minutes, stirring occasionally. Drain the liquid (or remove Matzo Balls from cooking liquid with a slotted spoon) and serve immediately or let cool to room temperature; transfer the Matzo Balls to a food storage container and refrigerate until ready to serve with the soup. Makes about 12 Matzo Balls.

Roasted Beets with Horseradish-Watercress Vinaigrette

8 medium beets, rinsed
¹/₄ cup canola oil
¹/₄ cup apple cider vinegar
1 tablespoon prepared horseradish
1¹/₂ teaspoons Dijon mustard
1 teaspoon brown sugar

¹/₂ teaspoon salt
¹/₂ teaspoon freshly ground black pepper
1 medium red onion, chopped
3 or 4 celery stalks, chopped
1 small bunch fresh watercress (about
4 ounces), trimmed and chopped

Helpful Hint:

If watercress is unavailable, substitute 3 or 4 tablespoons of chopped fresh dill or tarragon.

Preheat the oven to 375° F.

Wrap the beets in aluminum foil and place on a baking pan. Roast until the beets are tender, about 50 minutes to 1 hour. Remove the beets from the oven, unwrap, and let cool.

Meanwhile, in a large mixing bowl, whisk together the oil, vinegar, horseradish, mustard, brown sugar, salt, and pepper.

When the beets are cool enough to handle, peel off the skins. Coarsely chop the beets and add to the vinaigrette; stir to coat thoroughly. Add the onion, celery, and watercress, and stir to combine. Refrigerate for 4 hours before serving or overnight. Serve cold or at room temperature.

Makes 6 servings

Per Serving: 133 Calories; 2g Protein; 10g Fat; 11g Carbohydrates; 0mg Cholesterol; 289mg Sodium; 2g Fiber.

Spinach-Potato Kugel

4 cups grated potatoes, peeled if desired
1 medium zucchini, grated
2 large carrots, peeled and grated
1 medium yellow onion, grated
¼ cup matzo meal
2 large eggs, beaten
½ cup 1% or 2% milk

1 large red bell pepper, seeded and diced
Two 10-ounce packages chopped frozen
*   spinach, thawed and drained*
1 teaspoon salt
1 teaspoon freshly ground black pepper
1 cup shredded low-fat Swiss cheese or
*   low-fat mozzarella cheese*

Preheat the oven to 375° F.

Place the potatoes in a colander and squeeze out the excess liquid. In a large mixing bowl, combine the potatoes with all of the remaining ingredients (except the cheese) and mix well. Spoon the mixture into a 9 × 13–inch oiled casserole or pan. Bake until the crust is lightly browned, about 45 minutes. Sprinkle the cheese over the top and cover. Let stand for 5 to 10 minutes before serving.

Makes 6 servings

Per Serving: 251 Calories; 12g Protein; 7g Fat; 33g Carbohydrates; 73mg Cholesterol; 514mg Sodium; 7g Fiber.

Lemon-Dressed Asparagus

Juice of 1½ lemons
2 tablespoons olive oil, or to taste
½ teaspoon salt
½ teaspoon white pepper
2 pounds asparagus spears, trimmed
¼ cup chopped fresh parsley

In a large mixing bowl, whisk together the lemon juice, oil, salt, and white pepper; set aside.

Bring about 1 quart of water to a boil in a medium saucepan. Place the asparagus in the water and cook until tender, about 3 to 5 minutes; drain in a colander and cool slightly. (Alternatively, steam the asparagus until tender.)

Add asparagus to dressing and gently toss. Arrange the spears on an oval platter and top with the parsley. Serve alongside the Spinach-Potato Kugel (previous recipe).

Makes 6 servings

Per Serving: 80 Calories; 4g Protein; 5g Fat; 8g Carbohydrates; 0mg Cholesterol; 196mg Sodium; 3g Fiber.

Coco-Nut Macaroons

1 cup grated, sweetened coconut
1 cup sliced or slivered almonds, finely
  chopped
1/2 cup brown sugar
1/3 cup matzo meal or potato starch
1/4 heaping cup cocoa powder, sifted
3 large egg whites
Nonstick cooking spray

In a mixing bowl, combine the coconut, almonds, brown sugar, matzo meal or potato starch, and cocoa powder.

In a separate bowl, vigorously whisk the egg whites until a stiff peak forms. Gently fold the egg whites into the coconut mixture, forming a ball. Cover and refrigerate for 2 hours.

Preheat the oven to 325° F. Spray a cookie sheet with nonstick cooking spray or line it with a sheet of waxed paper. Drop the batter by the tablespoon onto the baking pan. Bake until the edges of the macaroons are firm, about 15 to 20 minutes. Remove from the oven and let cool to room temperature. Store in an airtight container until ready to serve. Makes 1 dozen cookies.

Per Cookie: 123 Calories; 3g Protein; 6g Fat; 14g Carbohydrates; 0mg Cholesterol; 20mg Sodium; 2g Fiber.

a
Rustic
Tuscan
Dinner

Ribollita • White Beans with Sun-Dried Tomatoes •

Asparagus and Mushroom Risotto • Wine-Braised Broccoli Rabe (Rapini) •

Chocolate-Coated Almond Biscotti

recipes make *6* servings

Asparagus and Mushroom Risotto (page 55) and Wine-Braised Broccoli Rabe (page 56)

*T*uscany is a region in Italy known for its rich culinary heritage. Olive oil, crusty bread, seasonal vegetables, pasta, rice, and beans form the pillars of Tuscan cuisine. The country fare is wholesome, high-spirited, and artfully seasoned with garlic, herbs, and spices. Tuscans know how to eat, so a menu based on Tuscan dishes is a natural for entertaining.

A dinner devoted to Tuscan cuisine begins with Ribollita, a hearty minestrone served over leftover bread. (*Ribollita* loosely means "twice boiled.") Tuscans are prodigious bean-eaters, so this menu features a helping of stewed White Beans with Sun-Dried Tomatoes.

The centerpiece of the meal is Asparagus and Mushroom Risotto, which is complemented by Wine-Braised Broccoli Rabe, also known as rapini, a leafy green vegetable with an assertive mustard flavor and a hint of broccoli.

Unlike most rice dishes, risotto yearns to be creamy, dense, and fluid—almost soupy—not fluffy and light like American rice. To achieve this texture, risotto is continuously stirred and simmered in a generous amount of liquid. The favored grain for risotto is arborio, a short-grain white rice that melds into a thick, chewy texture when cooked. Grated Parmesan cheese and garlic contribute to risotto's signature flavor.

Biscotti, a crunchy, twice-baked cookie, makes a light after-dinner treat. Chocolate-Covered Almond Biscotti are easy to make and are ideal for dunking in espresso or cappuccino.

This menu radiates with warm, wholesome flavors and stick-to-your-ribs sustenance. Saluto!

Kitchen Countdown

1 to 2 days before	Make the Chocolate-Coated Almond Biscotti.
1 day before	Make the Ribollita; transfer to a food storage container, cover, and refrigerate.
1½ hours before	Soak the dried tomatoes for the White Beans with Sun-Dried Tomatoes.
45 minutes before	Make the Asparagus and Mushroom Risotto. Reheat the Ribollita over low heat.
30 minutes before	Cook the White Beans with Sun-Dried Tomatoes.
15 to 20 minutes before	Prepare the Wine-Braised Broccoli Rabe.
Dinnertime	Serve the Ribollita as the first course. Arrange the Asparagus and Mushroom Risotto, Wine-Braised Broccoli Rabe, and White Beans with Sun-Dried Tomatoes on warm supper plates. Bring out the Chocolate-Coated Almond Biscotti with coffee at the finish.
What guests can bring	Frozen low-fat gelato to serve with the biscotti; or a bottle of Italian white wine.

Ribollita

1 tablespoon olive oil
1 medium yellow onion, diced
1 medium zucchini, diced
1 cup shredded red or white cabbage
2 cloves garlic, minced
7 cups water or vegetable stock
2 cups diced, white potatoes, peeled if
    desired
1½ tablespoons dried parsley
1 tablespoon dried oregano

1½ teaspoons dried basil
½ teaspoon salt
½ teaspoon freshly ground black pepper
One 28-ounce can whole tomatoes
¼ pound fresh green beans, cut into
    1-inch lengths
1 day-old loaf (about 1 pound) pumper-
    nickel or Italian bread, torn into
    bite-size pieces
1 cup grated Parmesan cheese (optional)

In a large saucepan or Dutch oven, heat the oil over medium-high heat. Add the onion, zucchini, cabbage, and garlic and cook, stirring, for 5 to 7 minutes. Stir in the water or stock, potatoes, parsley, oregano, basil, salt, and pepper, and cook for 10 minutes over medium heat. Add the tomatoes and cook for about 30 minutes more over medium-low heat, stirring occasionally. Stir in the green beans and cook until tender, about 5 minutes more.

Remove from the heat and let cool to room temperature. Cover and refrigerate for 4 hours or overnight.

To reheat, bring the soup to a simmer. Cook over medium heat for 10 to 15 minutes. Place the torn bread into the bottom of each soup bowl. Ladle the hot soup over the bread and pack it down with a spoon. Let the soup sit for a few minutes to allow the bread to soak up the flavors. Pass the Parmesan cheese at the table if desired.

Makes 6 servings

Per Serving: 305 Calories; 10g Protein; 5g Fat; 57g Carbohydrates; 0mg Cholesterol; 909mg Sodium; 9g Fiber.

White Beans with Sun-Dried Tomatoes

1½ cups sun-dried tomatoes (not oil
    packed)
1 tablespoon olive oil
1 large yellow onion, diced
2 or 3 cloves garlic, minced
Three 15-ounce cans cannellini beans,
    drained

¼ cup water
½ teaspoon ground sage
½ teaspoon salt
½ teaspoon freshly ground black pepper
¼ teaspoon dried red pepper flakes
⅓ cup chopped fresh basil

In a small bowl, soak the tomatoes in enough warm water to cover for about 1 hour; drain and coarsely chop.

In a saucepan, heat the oil over medium-high heat. Add the onion and garlic and cook, stirring, for about 4 minutes. Add the beans, tomatoes, water, sage, salt, pepper, and pepper flakes and cook over low heat, stirring frequently, for 10 to 15 minutes more. Stir in the basil and remove from the heat. Keep warm until ready to serve.

Makes 6 servings

Per Serving: 422 Calories; 20g Protein; 3g Fat; 76g Carbohydrates; 0mg Cholesterol; 224mg Sodium; 17g Fiber.

Asparagus and Mushroom Risotto

1 tablespoon olive oil
1 medium red onion, chopped
1 large red bell pepper, seeded and diced
8 ounces button mushrooms, thickly sliced
4 ounces oyster mushrooms or cremini mushrooms, thickly sliced
2 cloves garlic, minced
1¹/₂ cups arborio rice
4¹/₂ cups hot tap water

¹/₂ cup dry white wine
1¹/₂ tablespoons dried parsley, or 3 to 4 tablespoons fresh parsley, chopped
¹/₂ teaspoon salt
¹/₂ teaspoon white pepper
10 to 12 asparagus spears, trimmed and cut into 1-inch sections
¹/₄ cup plus 2 tablespoons grated Parmesan or Romano cheese

In a large saucepan, heat the oil over medium heat. Add the onion, bell pepper, mushrooms, and garlic. Cook for about 8 minutes, stirring frequently. Stir in the rice, 2 cups hot tap water, wine, parsley, salt, and white pepper and bring to a simmer over medium-high heat. Cook over low heat, uncovered, for about 10 minutes, stirring frequently.

Stir in the remaining 2¹/₂ cups water and asparagus. Cook, continuing to stir, until the rice is tender, about 10 to 12 minutes more.

Remove from the heat and fold in the cheese. Let stand for a few minutes before serving. Serve with warm Italian bread.

Makes 6 servings

Per Serving: 260 Calories; 7g Protein; 4g Fat; 45g Carbohydrates; 4mg Cholesterol; 278mg Sodium; 2g Fiber.

Wine-Braised Broccoli Rabe (Rapini)

2 medium bunches (about 2 pounds) broccoli rabe (see Helpful Hint)
2 tablespoons olive oil
2 or 3 cloves garlic, minced
¹/₄ cup dry white wine
Salt and pepper to taste

Remove the fibrous stems of the broccoli rabe, leaving just the small florets, and discard. Rinse the broccoli rabe in a colander and pat dry. Coarsely chop the leaves.

In a large, wide skillet, heat the oil over medium-high heat. Add the garlic and cook, stirring, for 2 to 3 minutes. Stir in the broccoli rabe and wine and cook over medium heat, stirring frequently, until the greens are wilted, about 5 to 7 minutes. Transfer to serving plates and season to taste with salt and pepper.

Makes *6* servings

Per Serving: 90 Calories; 5g Protein; 5g Fat; 8g Carbohydrates; 0mg Cholesterol; 130mg Sodium; 5g Fiber.

> **Helpful Hint:**
> Broccoli rabe, also called rapini, is a leafy green vegetable with miniature broccoli-like florets. It has a sharp mustard flavor and is extremely nutritious. Escarole, dandelion greens, or turnip greens may be substituted.

Chocolate-Coated Almond Biscotti

3 tablespoons canola oil
2 eggs
¹/₂ teaspoon almond extract
¹/₄ cup sugar
¹/₄ cup packed brown sugar
2 cups unbleached white flour

2 teaspoons baking powder
1¹/₄ cups slivered almonds, chopped
Nonstick cooking spray
Chocolate Coating for Biscotti
   (recipe follows)

Preheat the oven to 375° F.

In a large bowl, whisk together oil, eggs, and almond extract until fluffy. Stir in the sugars and beat until well blended.

In a separate mixing bowl, combine flour and baking powder. Gradually blend into the egg mixture. Fold in 1 cup of almonds. On a lightly floured surface, divide the dough in half and form 2 narrow logs about 12 inches long. Place the logs on a lightly sprayed baking sheet and pat down slightly until the logs are about 2 inches wide. Bake until firm and lightly browned, about 20 minutes.

Remove from the oven and let cool to room temperature. Slice the logs on the diagonal into ³/₄-inch-thick slices. Place the slices cut-side down on the baking sheet. Reduce the oven temperature to 325° F and bake for about 8 minutes; flip biscotti, and bake until crisp, 4 to 7 minutes more.

When biscotti are crisp, transfer to racks and cool to room temperature.

Prepare Chocolate Coating for Biscotti. Spread the chocolate coating over 1 side of the biscotti. Sprinkle the remaining almonds over the tops and press almonds into the coating. Store in an airtight container until ready to serve. Arrange on a platter and serve with a hot beverage.

Makes cookies

Per Cookie with Frosting: 92 Calories; 2g Protein; 4g Fat; 12g Carbohydrates; 11mg Cholesterol; 32mg Sodium; 0.9g Fiber.

Chocolate Coating for Biscotti

³/₄ cup semisweet chocolate chips
1 tablespoon amaretto or coffee liqueur
1 tablespoon canola oil

Combine all of the ingredients in the top of a double boiler. Stir constantly until completely melted.

Alternatively, microwave until melted, about 1¹/₂ to 2 minutes on high. (Stop after 1 minute to stir.) Keep warm until ready to use.

Makes about ¹/₂ cup

a Cinco de Mayo Celebration

Minty Guacamole • Frijoles Refritos • Pico de Gallo •

Sizzling Vegetable Fajitas • Apricot Rice Pudding

recipes make *4* to *6* servings

Sizzling Vegetable Fajitas (page 63), Minty Guacamole (page 62),
Pico de Gallo (page 63), Frijoles Refritos (page 62)

Cinco de Mayo is the commemoration of Mexico's victory over French invaders on May 5, 1862, near Mexico City. The holiday has since spread northward, and American bars and restaurants annually sponsor an abundance of Cinco de Mayo festivities. It is also an opportunity to celebrate the renaissance of Mexican cuisine. Mexican food has shed its taco-nacho stereotyped image (dripping with fat and hard to digest) and proven to be a real treasure of enlightened and savory fare.

This Cinco de Mayo buffet is adorned with a variety of south-of-the-border staples enhanced with New World tastes. For starters, there is Minty Guacamole, a luscious, creamy purée of avocados and assertive spices. For this mint-scented guacamole (or any other guacamole, for that matter), it is important to use ripe avocados. You can determine the degree of ripeness by the holding the avocado in the base of your hand and gently pressing down with your thumb—it should give a little. A good guacamole is the crème de la crème of vegetable dips.

Also on the menu is a lively, palate-stimulating Pico de Gallo. This fresh tomato salsa is enlivened with the dynamic trio of classic Mexican ingredients: fresh lime, chile peppers, and pungent cilantro. Joining the salsa is another tried-and-true dish, Frijoles Refritos, also known as refried beans, although in this case, *well cooked* more closely describes the dish—there's no deep-fat frying involved. The beans are cooked, spiced, mashed, and stirred, and cooked again in the skillet.

Sizzling Vegetable Fajitas form the heart and soul of this fiesta buffet. While it seems that there are hundreds of recipes for fajitas these days, this version captures the rustic, smoky nuances of Tex-Mex cooking. Strips of vegetables are infused with lime, (vegetarian) Worcestershire sauce, garlic, and oregano, and roasted until tender.

The vegetable medley is accompanied with the traditional fajitas entourage of flour tortillas, romaine lettuce (more healthful than iceberg), and shredded cheese. Guests should be encouraged to fill their tortillas with a sampling from each of the dishes.

Such an eclectic spread deserves a soothing dessert with a hint of charm. Thus said, Apricot Rice Pudding is the perfect exclamation point to finish up this meal. It is a fruitier, lighter version of one of Mexico's most cherished desserts, *arroz con leche*.

Kitchen Countdown

2 to 3 days before	Shop for avocados. If only unripe avocados are available, store in a paper bag at room temperature for a couple of days until fully ripened.
1 day before	Make the Apricot Rice Pudding and refrigerate.
2 hours before	Make the Pico de Gallo.
1 to 2 hours before	Make the Minty Guacamole.
30 to 45 minutes before	Roast the vegetables for the Sizzling Vegetable Fajitas.
15 minutes before	Cook the pinto beans for Frijoles Refritos. Shred or chiffonade the lettuce for the Sizzling Vegetable Fajitas.
Dinnertime	Serve the food buffet-style. Place all of the menu items in serving bowls and arrange on a round table. At the last minute, warm the tortillas over a hot burner or grill. Place in a tortilla warmer or round dish and cover; set on the serving table. When the Sizzling Vegetable Fajitas are done, the meal begins. Bring out the rice pudding after all of the plates have been cleaned.
What guests can bring	Tapes or compact discs of mariachi music (Mexican folk music); ingredients for margaritas or daiquiris; tequila.

Minty Guacamole

3 or 4 ripe avocados, peeled, pitted and
    chopped
1 large ripe tomato, diced
$^1/_3$ cup finely chopped red onion
2 cloves garlic, minced
2 tablespoons chopped fresh mint

Juice of 1 lime
$^1/_2$ teaspoon ground cumin
$^1/_2$ teaspoon salt
$^1/_2$ teaspoon freshly ground black pepper
2 whole scallions, chopped for garnish

Place all of the ingredients except the scallions in a food processor fitted
with a steel blade and process for about 10 seconds. Alternatively, mash
the ingredients by hand in a mixing bowl, forming a chunky paste.
Transfer to a serving bowl and top with the scallions. Serve with Sizzling
Vegetable Fajitas (below).

Makes about 4 cups

Per $^1/_4$ Cup: 62 Calories; 1g Protein; 6g Fat; 3g Carbohydrates; 0mg Cholesterol;
71mg Sodium; 1g Fiber.

Frijoles Refritos

Two 15-ounce cans pinto beans
2 teaspoons canola oil
1 medium yellow onion, chopped
1 large clove garlic, minced

1 jalapeño pepper, seeded and minced
    (optional)
1 teaspoon ground cumin
$^1/_4$ teaspoon freshly ground black pepper
2 tablespoons chopped fresh parsley

Drain the beans, reserving about $^1/_2$ cup of the bean liquid. Set aside.

In a medium saucepan, heat the oil over medium-high heat. Add the
onion, garlic, and jalapeño if desired and cook, stirring, for 2 to 3 minutes. Stir in the beans, half of the reserved bean liquid, cumin, and
pepper. Cook over low heat for 5 to 10 minutes, stirring frequently,
mashing the beans with the back of a spoon. Add more reserved bean
liquid if the beans become too dry.

Remove the beans from the heat and stir in the parsley. Serve
immediately, or keep warm until ready to eat. Serve with Sizzling
Vegetable Fajitas (below).

Makes 4 servings

Per Serving: 206 Calories; 10g Protein; 3g Fat; 35g Carbohydrates; 0mg Cholesterol;
887mg Sodium; 8g Fiber.

Pico de Gallo

3 or 4 ripe tomatoes, diced
1/3 cup chopped red onion
1 red bell pepper, seeded and diced
1/2 cup peeled and diced jícama (optional)
1 or 2 jalapeño or serrano chiles, seeded and minced
2 tablespoons chopped cilantro
Juice of 1 lime

Combine all of the ingredients in a medium mixing bowl. Refrigerate for at least 1 hour before serving. Serve with Sizzling Vegetable Fajitas (below).

Makes about 3 cups

Per 1/4 Cup: 7 Calories; 1g Protein; 0.1g Fat; 2g Carbohydrates; 0mg Cholesterol; 33mg Sodium; 0.4g Fiber.

Helpful Hint:

Jícama, also called Mexican potato, is a tan-skinned, rotund, turnip-shaped tuber with a crisp, moist flesh and water chestnut flavor. Look for it in the specialty produce section of most supermarkets or in Mexican markets.

Sizzling Vegetable Fajitas

Marinade

4 cloves garlic, minced
1/2 cup vegetarian Worcestershire sauce
1/2 cup low-sodium or regular soy sauce
1/4 cup fresh lime juice
1/4 cup canola oil
1 tablespoon brown sugar
1 tablespoon dried oregano

Vegetables

1 medium eggplant, halved crosswise and cut into 1/2-inch-wide strips
1 large zucchini, halved crosswise and cut into 1/2-inch-wide strips
2 red or green bell peppers, seeded and cut into 1/2-inch-wide strips
1 large yellow onion, cut into 1/2-inch-wide strips

Helpful Hint:

There are several brands of Worcestershire sauce on the market that do not contain anchovies. Check the labels of the brands in your super-market or natural food store to find a vegetarian version.

To make the marinade, combine all of the marinade ingredients in a mixing bowl.

Place all of the vegetable ingredients in a shallow casserole dish and cover with the marinade. Refrigerate for 2 hours. Baste the vegetables after 1 hour.

Preheat the oven to 400° F.

(continues)

Using tongs, place the vegetables on a large ovenproof skillet or 2 fajita skillets. Place in the oven and roast until the vegetables are tender, about 15 to 20 minutes. Baste the vegetables with the marinade after about 10 minutes. Remove from the heat and arrange on a large serving platter. Serve buffet-style with all of the Fajitas Accompaniments (see below).

Makes *12* servings

Per Serving: 141 Calories; 4g Protein; 5g Fat; 22g Carbohydrates; 0mg Cholesterol; 525mg Sodium; 6g Fiber.

FAJITAS ACCOMPANIMENTS

Frijoles Refritos (page 62)

Pico de Gallo (page 63)

Minty Guacamole (page 62)

2 cups shredded low-fat or regular Monterey jack cheese

1 medium head romaine lettuce, rinsed and cut into ribbons (chiffonade)

Twelve 6-inch flour tortillas

Apricot Rice Pudding

3 cups milk or rice milk
3 cups cooked short-grain rice
     (about 1¹/₄ cups raw)
¹/₂ cup sugar
2 tablespoons honey
1 cup chopped dried apricots
¹/₄ cup golden raisins

¹/₂ teaspoon vanilla or almond extract
1 cinnamon stick (or ¹/₄ teaspoon ground)
One 3-inch strip orange peel
3 tablespoons (approximately) grated
     sweetened coconut
Strips of orange peel for garnish

Combine all of the ingredients except orange peel in a medium saucepan. Over low heat, cook, stirring occasionally, until the mixture thickens, about 20 to 25 minutes. Remove from the heat and let cool slightly. Transfer to a food storage container, cover, and refrigerate overnight.

When ready to serve, remove the cinnamon stick and orange peel and scoop the pudding into bowls with an ice cream scooper. Garnish with strips of orange peel.

Helpful Hint:
Arborio rice (of risotto fame) makes a creamy, luscious rice pudding.

Makes about *6* servings

Per Serving: 358 Calories; 7g Protein; 5g Fat; 72g Carbohydrates; 17mg Cholesterol; 64mg Sodium; 3g Fiber.

a *Medley of* Mediterranean *Flavors*

Caldo Gallego • Greek Salad with Feta Vinaigrette • Beet Ratatouille •

Scallion Couscous • Poached Summer Fruit in Red Wine

recipes make *8* to *10* servings

Beet Ratatouille (page 71), Scallion Couscous (page 72), and peaches and a bottle of wine for making Poached Summer Fruit in Red Wine (page 72)

Naturally healthful and vibrantly flavored, Mediterranean cooking is fertile terrain for the vegetarian palate. A bounty of seasonal vegetables, legumes, grains, and herbs appear prominently on the center of the Mediterranean dinner plate, not as secondary dishes on the side. Garlic, olive oil, and vinegar are used with gusto and provide a mellifluous blend of signature flavors.

Supper begins with Caldo Gallego, a hearty Galatian soup of potatoes, greens, white beans, and parsley. A verdant and unintimidating Greek Salad with Feta Vinaigrette combines spinach, raw vegetables, and a vinaigrette sated with feta cheese. The main course, Beet Ratatouille, is a magenta-hued improvisation on the classic Mediterranean vegetable stew. The ratatouille is served with a mound of fluffy, quick-to-prepare Scallion Couscous.

For a colorful and well-rounded plate presentation, arrange the salad, ratatouille, and couscous together on the same plate. Pass a carafe of red wine or sangria at the table. Think sunshine: Fill an elegant vase with brilliant sunflowers for a centerpiece. Set the mood with instrumental music featuring Spanish guitars.

A Mediterranean meal would be incomplete without a fruit-inspired finale. To this end, Poached Summer Fruit in Red Wine, wine-poached peaches and nectarines, makes an exquisite dessert. A scoop of low-fat yogurt balances the tanginess of the fruit and adds a pleasing finishing touch.

If you are in the mood for a dinner party with an accent on light and healthful tastes, this Mediterranean menu may be the answer. It will leave you and your guests with a renewed appreciation for the sun-drenched flavors of Mediterranean dining.

Kitchen Countdown

1 day before	Poach the fruit and make the red wine sauce for the Poached Summer Fruit in Red Wine; cover and store separately in refrigerator. Make the vinaigrette for the Greek Salad with Feta Vinaigrette and refrigerate.
2 to 3 hours before (or the day before)	Prepare Caldo Gallego. If prepared the day before, cool to room temperature, cover, and refrigerate. About 1 hour before dinner, reheat over low heat.
2 to 3 hours before	Prepare rest of ingredients for Greek Salad with Feta Vinaigrette.
1½ to 2 hours before	Roast the beets for the Beet Ratatouille.
30 to 45 minutes before	Finish the Beet Ratatouille. Toss the salad.
20 minutes before	Prepare Scallion Couscous.
Dinnertime	For the first course, serve the Caldo Gallego in large, warm tureens. Place the Greek Spinach Salad, Beet Ratatouille, and Scallion Couscous on dinner plates; serve the feta dressing on the side in a small pitcher with a spoon. After dinner, arrange the poached fruit on dessert plates, drizzle with the red wine sauce, and garnish with mint before serving.
What guests can bring	A loaf or two of whole-grain, rustic bread for the soup, or a dessert wine.

Caldo Gallego

1 tablespoon olive oil
1 large yellow onion, chopped
4 cloves garlic, minced
1 red bell pepper, seeded and diced
8 cups water
6 cups diced white potatoes, peeled
    or unpeeled
1 teaspoon salt

3/4 teaspoon ground white pepper or
    black pepper
6 cups chopped, packed fresh turnip
    greens or kale (about 1 large bunch)
Two 15-ounce cans white kidney beans,
    drained
1/2 cup chopped fresh parsley
1 cup grated Parmesan cheese (optional)

Heat the oil in a large saucepan over medium heat and add the onion, garlic, and bell pepper. Cook, stirring, for about 5 minutes. Add the water, potatoes, salt, and pepper, and bring to a simmer. Cook over medium-low heat, stirring occasionally, until potatoes are tender, about 20 minutes.

Stir in the turnip greens or kale, beans, and parsley. Cook for 10 to 15 minutes more over low heat. To thicken, mash the potatoes against the side of the pan with a wooden spoon. Turn off the heat and let sit, uncovered, for 10 to 15 minutes on the stovetop before serving.

Ladle the soup into bowls and sprinkle with Parmesan if desired. Serve with warm bread.

Makes 8 servings

Per Serving: 219 Calories; 9g Protein; 2g Fat; 43g Carbohydrates; 0mg Cholesterol; 659mg Sodium; 9g Fiber.

Greek Salad with Feta Vinaigrette

Vinaigrette

1 1/3 cup olive oil or canola oil
2/3 cup red wine vinegar
1 1/2 teaspoons Dijon mustard
1/4 cup chopped fresh mint
    (1 tablespoon dried)
2 teaspoons dried oregano
1/2 teaspoon dried thyme
1/2 teaspoon freshly ground black pepper
1/3 pound feta cheese, crumbled
1 large clove garlic, minced

Salad

One 10-ounce package fresh spinach,
    trimmed of stems and rinsed
1 medium head romaine lettuce
10 to 12 button mushrooms, sliced
2 large tomatoes, cut into eighths
2 medium carrots, peeled and grated
1 medium cucumber, peeled and sliced
    crosswise
1 medium red onion, thinly sliced

To make the vinaigrette, in a mixing bowl, whisk together the oil, vinegar, mustard, mint, oregano, thyme, and pepper. Blend in the feta cheese and garlic. Cover and refrigerate for 2 hours or overnight.

For the salad, coarsely chop or tear the spinach and romaine leaves by hand. In a large salad bowl, toss the greens with the mushrooms, tomatoes, carrots, cucumber, and red onion. Refrigerate until ready to serve.

To serve, place salad on serving plates; whisk dressing and serve on the side.

Makes *8* servings

Per Serving with 1 Tablespoon Vinaigrette: 106 Calories; 4g Protein; 7g Fat; 10g Carbohydrates; 3mg Cholesterol; 79mg Sodium; 3g Fiber.

Beet Ratatouille

4 medium beets, scrubbed
1½ tablespoons olive oil
1 large yellow onion, diced
4 cups diced eggplant (about 1 medium)
2 medium yellow summer squash or zucchini, diced
2 large cloves garlic, minced

One 28-ounce can stewed tomatoes
1½ tablespoons dried oregano
1 tablespoon dried basil
1 teaspoon salt
½ teaspoon freshly ground black pepper
One 15-ounce can red kidney beans, drained

Preheat the oven to 375° F.

Wrap the beets in aluminum foil and place on a baking pan. Roast until beets are tender, about 50 minutes to 1 hour. Remove the beets from the oven, unwrap, and let cool. Peel off any loose skin. Coarsely chop the beets and set aside.

Meanwhile, heat the oil in a large saucepan over medium heat. Add the onion, eggplant, squash, and garlic. Cook for about 10 minutes, stirring occasionally. Stir in the tomatoes, oregano, basil, salt, and pepper, and cook over medium-low heat for 15 minutes more, stirring occasionally. Stir in the beets and beans and cook for 5 to 10 minutes more over low heat.

Serve with the Scallion Couscous (recipe follows).

Makes *8* servings

Per Serving: 145 Calories; 6g Protein; 3g Fat; 26g Carbohydrates; 0mg Cholesterol; 723mg Sodium; 9g Fiber.

Scallion Couscous

3 cups couscous
4½ cups boiling water
4 or 5 large whole scallions, trimmed
   and chopped

¼ cup chopped fresh parsley
½ teaspoon salt
½ teaspoon ground black pepper
Juice of 1 large lemon

Combine all ingredients in a large bowl or pan. Cover and let stand for
15 minutes.

Fluff the couscous with a fork. Serve with the Beet Ratatouille
(previous recipe).

Makes *8* servings

Per Serving: 277 Calories; 9g Protein; 0g Fat; 60g Carbohydrates; 0mg Cholesterol;
147mg Sodium; 1g Fiber.

Poached Summer Fruit in Red Wine

1 bottle dry red wine, such as cabernet
   sauvignon or burgundy
⅓ cup honey
¼ teaspoon ground cinnamon
2 black peppercorns
1-inch strip lemon zest

4 or 5 ripe peaches
4 or 5 ripe nectarines
24 ounces low-fat plain or vanilla yogurt
8 to 12 extra-large strawberries (optional)
1 small bunch fresh mint leaves for
   garnish

In a large saucepan, combine the wine, honey, cinnamon, peppercorns,
and lemon zest and bring to a simmer. Add the peaches and nectarines
to the pan and return to a simmer. Cook over low heat until the fruit is
tender, about 8 to 12 minutes.

With a slotted spoon, transfer fruit to a shallow bowl. Let the fruit cool
for a few minutes and then cover and refrigerate for 2 hours or overnight.

Simmer the poaching liquid over medium-high heat, stirring frequently,
until the sauce is syrupy and reduced by about half, about 10 minutes.
Remove from the heat and let cool for a few minutes. Cover and refrigerate for 2 hours or overnight.

To serve, arrange fruit on small plates. Drizzle the wine sauce over
the fruit and spoon a dollop of yogurt on the side. Place a strawberry
in the center of the yogurt. Garnish with mint leaves.

Makes *8* servings

Per Serving: 230 Calories; 6g Protein; 2g Fat; 32g Carbohydrates; 5mg Cholesterol;
66mg Sodium; 2g Fiber.

Vegetarian *Wedding* Bells

Focaccia with Sun-Dried Tomatoes • Asparagus and Red Potato Salad •

Roasted Tricolor Sweet Peppers • Wild Rice and Vegetable Paella •

Exotic Bean and Corn Medley • Pineapple-Carrot Wedding Cake

makes *30* servings

Pineapple-Carrot Wedding Cake (page 82)

*A*t last, a vegetarian wedding menu. What better way to celebrate such a monumental occasion than to treat your guests to a grand display of vegetarian cuisine. Traditionally, wedding receptions have been a sorry refuge for staid stuffed chicken and cold slabs of beef. Often it is a day to remember but a meal to forget. This vegetarian menu departs from the past with great culinary gusto.

Granted, like most couples you will not physically prepare the wedding banquet, especially in light of the mountain of nuptial details. Although you may rely on a caterer or restaurant staff for the meal, you can still take an active role in the menu planning. With that in mind, this wedding menu is intended to pique your interest in the enticing possibilities of an all-vegetarian wedding menu.

The picturesque spread begins with Focaccia with Sun-Dried Tomatoes, a flat round bread with a thick, chewy texture and authentic Italian taste. (It is said that when a pizza dreams, it dreams of becoming a focaccia.) These minifocaccias are topped with sun-dried tomatoes, garlic, and olive oil and are served as individual portions.

The Asparagus and Red Potato Salad is a light and crunchy combination of red potatoes, regal asparagus, herbs, and a coat of vinaigrette-style dressing. Unlike most potato or vegetable salads, this enlightened salad is free of heavy mayonnaise or egg-based dressings; it also retains a firm, not mushy, texture.

For a side dish, there is a colorful mélange of Roasted Tricolor Sweet Peppers, strips of tender yellow, red, and green bell peppers presented on a sizzling platter. Also appearing in a supporting role is the Exotic Bean and Corn Medley, an enlightened assortment of heirloom beans (such as Anasazi, Appaloosa, and Jacob's cattle) blended with corn and hominy, a chewy, puffed-up corn kernel. Heirloom beans retain their unique speckled markings when cooked and are saved for special occasions such as this.

For the entrée, Wild Rice and Vegetable Paella is a hearty combination of wild rice, brown rice, vegetables, and fragrant spices. It is natural for rice to command center stage at a wedding dinner; in many parts of the world, rice symbolizes prosperity and good fortune. The tossing of rice at newlywed couples is seen as an expression of goodwill. For this celebration—an apex of life—a rice-inspired entrée signifies warm sentiments, festive symbolism, and savory flavors.

There seems to be a mystery surrounding the wedding cake—what kind of cake can be stacked so high? Actually, almost any cake can be adapted to a wedding cake recipe. Of course, for the actual preparation, it is probably a wise idea to seek out an experienced pastry chef. However, it helps to have a cake recipe in mind, one that you've tasted and enjoyed. This Pineapple-Carrot Wedding Cake should kindle your interest. It is filled with tropical pineapple, carrots, nuts, and raisins, and fragrantly spiced with nutmeg and cinnamon.

1 or 2 days before the wedding	Bake the Pineapple-Carrot Wedding Cake.
1 day before	Bake the Focaccia with Sun-Dried Tomatoes. Soak the beans for the Exotic Bean and Corn Medley.
The morning of the wedding	Prepare the Asparagus and Red Potato Salad and refrigerate.
2 to 3 hours before	Prepare the Exotic Bean and Corn Medley.
1½ hours before	Make the Wild Rice and Vegetable Paella.
45 minutes before	Prepare the Roasted Tricolor Sweet Peppers.
Dinnertime	Set up the buffet table and transfer the Wild Rice and Vegetable Paella, Roasted Tricolor Sweet Peppers, and Exotic Bean and Corn Medley to steam tables. Serve the Asparagus and Red Potato Salad in a large bowl. Pile the Focaccia with Sun-Dried Tomatoes on a large platter. Bring the wedding cake out at the finish.
What guests can bring	Dancing shoes. Champagne bottles with personalized labels would be a nice touch. Gifts, naturally.

Focaccia with Sun-Dried Tomatoes

Dough

7 cups hot tap water (between 110° F
    and 115° F)
4 teaspoons active dry yeast
17 to 18 cups unbleached white flour
1⅓ cups olive oil
2 tablespoons plus 2 teaspoons salt

Topping

2 cups sun-dried tomatoes (not oil-packed)
¾ cup olive oil
8 cloves garlic, minced
¼ cup mixture of chopped fresh herbs
    (including basil, rosemary, thyme,
    and oregano)
1½ teaspoons salt
1½ teaspoons pepper
Cornmeal for dusting baking pans, or
    parchment paper

Variation:

For a whole-wheat focaccia, substitute 8 cups whole-wheat flour for the 8 cups white flour.

To make the dough, combine the water and yeast in a large mixing bowl. Let stand until foamy, about 10 minutes. Whisk the liquid until the yeast is dissolved. Gradually mix in the flour, 1⅓ cups oil, and salt, forming a moist, soft dough. Knead the dough with floured hands (or in an electric mixer fitted with a dough hook) for about 10 minutes. Form 4 large balls and place in lightly oiled mixing bowls. Coat the balls of dough with the oil by rolling them around in the bowls. Cover the dough with plastic wrap and allow to rise until doubled, about 2 to 3 hours.

Punch down the balls and knead until the dough is elastic, about 1 to 2 minutes. Form into 4 balls again and return them to the oiled mixing bowls. Cover with the plastic wrap and let rise a second time until doubled, about 2 to 3 hours more.

To make the topping, soak the sun-dried tomatoes in warm water to cover for about 1 hour. Drain, discard the liquid, and coarsely chop the tomatoes. In medium mixing bowl, combine the tomatoes, ½ cup oil, garlic, herbs, salt, and pepper. Set aside.

Preheat the oven to 400° F. Lightly dust 5 or 6 large baking pans with cornmeal or line them with parchment paper. With floured hands, divide the dough into 32 baseball-sized balls. Flatten each ball into a 4-inch round and arrange on the baking pans.

Using a soup spoon, press a little less than 1 tablespoon of topping into the center of each round. With the back of the spoon, "brush" the sides of the rounds with the remaining ¼ cup olive oil. Place the pans in the oven and bake until the focaccias are lightly browned on bottom, about 20 minutes.

Remove the pans from the oven and cool on a rack. Store as you would homemade bread until ready to serve.

Makes *32* 4-inch focaccia

Per Serving: 357 Calories; 7g Protein; 13g Fat; 51g Carbohydrates; 0mg Cholesterol; 611mg Sodium; 4g Fiber.

Asparagus and Red Potato Salad

20 cups unpeeled, coarsely chopped red
    potatoes (20 to 24 medium potatoes)
50 to 60 asparagus spears, trimmed and
    cut into 1-inch pieces
2 cups canola oil
³/₄ cup apple cider vinegar or red wine
    vinegar
¹/₄ cup balsamic vinegar

¹/₄ cup Dijon mustard
³/₄ to 1 cup chopped fresh parsley
2 tablespoons celery seeds
1 tablespoon salt
1 tablespoon pepper
5 or 6 small red onions, thinly sliced
1 large bunch celery (core and leaves
    removed), finely chopped

In a large saucepan, place the potatoes in boiling water to cover and cook
over medium-high heat until easily pierced by a fork, about 15 minutes.
Drain in a colander and cool under cold running water.

    In another large saucepan, place the asparagus in boiling water to
cover and cook over medium-high heat until tender, about 5 minutes.
Drain in a colander and cool under cold running water.

    Meanwhile, in a large mixing bowl, whisk together the oil, vinegars,
mustard, parsley, celery seeds, salt, and pepper. Fold in the red onions
and celery. Then fold in potatoes and asparagus and toss. Cover and chill
for 3 or 4 hours before serving.

Makes *30* servings

Per Serving: 241 Calories; 2g Protein; 14g Fat; 24g Carbohydrates; 0mg Cholesterol;
289mg Sodium; 3g Fiber.

Roasted Tricolor Sweet Peppers

3 cups olive oil
1¹/₂ cups fresh lemon juice (from 6 to
    8 lemons)
10 to 12 cloves garlic, minced
1¹/₂ cups chopped fresh parsley
2 teaspoons ground cumin
1 tablespoon salt
2¹/₂ to 3 teaspoons freshly ground black
    pepper

24 to 28 red, green, and yellow bell
    peppers, seeded and cut into
    ¹/₂-inch-wide strips
2¹/₂ pounds button mushrooms, halved
    vertically (small ones kept whole)
6 medium red onions, peeled and sliced
    about ¹/₂ inch thick

Preheat the oven to 375° F.

    In a large mixing bowl, combine the oil, lemon juice, garlic, parsley,
cumin, salt, and pepper. Set aside.

(continues)

Arrange the peppers, mushrooms, and onions on large, lightly greased baking sheets. Roast the vegetables until tender, about 20 to 25 minutes. Using tongs, turn the vegetables after about 10 minutes.

Remove the vegetables from the oven and let cool slightly. Toss together with the oil-lemon mixture and let stand for 10 to 15 minutes before serving. If serving a buffet, transfer the dish to a steam table.

Makes *30* servings

Per Serving: 87 Calories; 1g Protein; 5g Fat; 7g Carbohydrates; 0mg Cholesterol; 60mg Sodium; 2g Fiber.

Wild Rice and Vegetable Paella

½ cup canola oil
5 or 6 medium yellow onions, diced
5 or 6 medium zucchini, diced
3 medium eggplant, diced
8 to 10 cloves garlic, minced
6½ quarts (approximately) water or
*   vegetable stock*
9 cups long- or medium-grain brown rice
3 cups wild rice

12 large carrots, peeled and diced
¼ cup dried oregano
3 tablespoons dried thyme leaves
4½ teaspoons salt
4½ teaspoons pepper
1 tablespoon ground turmeric
6 cups green peas, fresh or frozen
*   and thawed*

Preheat the oven to 375° F.

In an extremely large saucepan, heat the oil over medium heat. Add the onions, zucchini, eggplant, and garlic, and cook, stirring frequently, until the vegetables are tender, about 10 to 15 minutes.

Stir in the water or stock, both rices, carrots, oregano, thyme, salt, pepper, and turmeric, and bring to a simmer. Transfer the mixture to 2 or 3 large casseroles or deep baking pans. Cover and bake for 40 minutes.

Remove the paella from the oven, fluff the rice with a fork, and stir in the peas. Return to the oven and bake for 5 minutes more.

Remove the paella from the oven, fluff again, and let stand, covered, for about 15 minutes. If serving a buffet, transfer the paella to a steam table. Keep warm until ready to serve.

Makes *30* servings

Per Serving: 299 Calories; 6g Protein; 5g Fat; 58g Carbohydrates; 0mg Cholesterol; 434mg Sodium; 5g Fiber.

Exotic Bean and Corn Medley

7 cups heirloom beans (see Helpful Hint),
    soaked overnight and drained
8 to 10 quarts water
1/2 cup canola oil
7 medium yellow onions, diced
14 cloves garlic, minced
8 cups corn kernels (fresh or frozen)

6 cups canned hominy kernels (see
    Helpful Hint)
3 tablespoons dried oregano
2 tablespoons dried thyme
3 1/2 teaspoons salt
3 1/2 teaspoons freshly ground black
    pepper

In a very large saucepan, combine the beans and water and bring to a
simmer. Cook uncovered over medium-low heat until the beans are tender,
about 1 1/2 to 2 hours. Remove from the heat and let cool slightly; drain.

In another large saucepan, heat the oil over medium heat. Add the
onions and garlic and cook, stirring, for 4 minutes. Stir in the cooked
beans and all remaining ingredients, and cook uncovered for 8 to
10 minutes more over low heat, stirring occasionally. Keep warm until
ready to serve. If serving a buffet, transfer to a steam table.

Makes *30* servings

*Per Serving: 286 Calories; 13g Protein; 4g Fat; 50g Carbohydrates; 0mg Cholesterol;
261mg Sodium; 10g Fiber.*

Helpful Hint:

Exotic beans such as Anasazi,
Appaloosa, Jacob's cattle, and
calypso can be found in
gourmet food stores, well-
stocked supermarkets, and
natural food stores.

Canned hominy is available
in most well-stocked grocery
stores in the canned vegetable
section. If using dried hominy,
the kernels must be cooked
for about three hours before
adding to the recipe (follow
the package instructions).

Pineapple-Carrot Wedding Cake

2 cups canola oil
1 cup orange juice
2 cups sugar
2 cups brown sugar
4 large eggs
4 cups unbleached white flour
4 teaspoons baking powder
2 teaspoons ground cinnamon
2 teaspoons ground nutmeg
1½ teaspoons salt
4 cups peeled, grated carrots
2 cups finely diced pineapple (fresh or
    canned), drained if canned
2 cups diced walnuts
1½ cups raisins

Yogurt Cream Cheese Frosting

1 cup nonfat or low-fat plain yogurt
1 pound low-fat or nonfat whipped
    cream cheese
12 ounces confectioners' sugar
1 teaspoon fresh lemon juice
Edible fresh flowers (such as nasturtiums)
    for garnish

Preheat the oven to 350° F.

In a large mixing bowl, whisk together the oil, juice, and sugars. Add the eggs and whisk until the batter is light and creamy.

In a separate bowl, combine the flour, baking powder, cinnamon, nutmeg, and salt. Fold the dry mixture into the liquid ingredients to form a batter. Fold in the carrots, pineapple, walnuts, and raisins.

Pour the batter into a lightly greased 12 × 18–inch sheet pan with 2-inch-high sides. Place the pan in the oven on the middle rack and bake until a toothpick inserted in the center comes out clean, about 50 minutes to 1 hour. Cool to room temperature.

Cover the cake with aluminum foil and refrigerate until ready to frost with Yogurt Cream Cheese Frosting.

Blend all of the frosting ingredients together in a blender or with a whisk until creamy. Refrigerate until ready to ice the cake.

After the cake is frosted, arrange the edible flowers around the edges of the cake in a decorative fashion.

Makes about 54 2 × 2–inch pieces

Per Serving with Frosting: 267 Calories; 3g Protein; 13g Fat; 34g Carbohydrates; 28mg Cholesterol; 141mg Sodium; 1g Fiber.

> **Helpful Hint:**
> This cake also can be served at any festive celebration or occasion. To make a 10-inch round cake in a springform pan, cut all of the ingredients for cake and frosting in half.

all-American
Fourth of July
Picnic

Louisiana Red Bean and Rice Salad • Heartland Barbecued

Corn-on-the-Cob • California Grilled Vegetable and Tofu Kebabs •

Southwestern Jícama Coleslaw • Georgia Peach Tree Cobbler

recipes make 6 to 8 servings

California Grilled Vegetable and Tofu Kebabs (page 89) and Louisiana Red Bean and Rice Salad (page 88)

Although the Fourth of July is a celebration of our country's independence, it also marks the *real* beginning of summer. It is a time for barbecues, picnics, softball games, and myriad outdoor activities. Schools are out, vacations are in, there are fireworks and bands playing nearby, and the scent of backyard cookouts fills the air. Summer is now officially open.

With a sense of summery fun and adventure, this patriotic menu pays tribute to our country's quilted culinary heritage. From Louisiana territory, there is a piquant Louisiana Red Bean and Rice Salad, a spin on the classic Cajun combination. This hearty salad wonderfully complements the main course of California Vegetable and Tofu Kebabs, a skewer of grilled and basted vegetable and tofu, whose origins are rooted in California cuisine. Also appearing on the plate: Southwestern Jícama Coleslaw, southwestern-style slaw of jícama, cilantro, red cabbage, and carrots.

Any Fourth of July picnic would be woefully incomplete without corn-on-the-cob. Whether it is from a local farm stand or the nation's "Corn Belt," Heartland Barbecued Corn-on-the-Cob symbolizes the convivial spirit of summer entertaining. And instead of dripping in butter, this grilled version needs only a light basting of fresh lime to enhance its succulent kernels.

For dessert, there is a tantalizing Georgia Peach Tree Cobbler, a bona fide national treasure (if it hasn't been already, it should be registered as such). This delectable country treat will leave you wishing that the Fourth of July came more than once a year.

Kitchen Countdown

4 hours or 1 day before	Make the Louisiana Red Bean and Rice Salad.
3 hours before	Make the Southwestern Jícama Coleslaw. Mix the marinade for the California Grilled Vegetable and Tofu Kebabs.
2 to 3 hours before	Roast the tofu for the kebabs.
2 hours before	Make the Georgia Peach Tree Cobbler. (This also can be prepared up to 1 day ahead, refrigerated, and served cold or warmed up in the oven.)
1 hour before	Skewer the vegetables and tofu for the kebabs.
30 minutes before	Grill the corn.
15 to 30 minutes before	Grill the kebabs.
Dinnertime	Place all of the dishes on a large picnic table and let the guests serve themselves. The serving plates should be large enough to hold a good taste of everything. After dinner, serve the peach cobbler with scoops of frozen yogurt.
What guests can bring	Frozen yogurt to serve with the cobbler. Patriotic music, such as a vintage record of Kate Smith singing "God Bless America," or Tchaikovsky's *1812 Overture*.

Louisiana Red Bean and Rice Salad

1¹/₂ cups long-grain white or brown rice
3 to 3¹/₂ cups water
Two 15-ounce cans red kidney beans,
  drained
4 large or 6 medium scallions, chopped
2 medium ripe tomatoes, diced
1 medium cucumber, diced (peeled
  if waxed)
2 cloves garlic, minced

3 to 4 tablespoons canola oil
2 tablespoons red wine vinegar
¹/₄ cup chopped fresh parsley
2¹/₂ teaspoons dried oregano
1 teaspoon dried thyme
³/₄ teaspoon salt
¹/₂ teaspoon freshly ground black pepper
1 to 2 teaspoons hot pepper sauce

In a medium saucepan, combine the rice and 3 cups water and bring to a simmer. Cover and cook for 15 to 20 minutes over low heat, until all of the water is absorbed. If using brown rice, add about ¹/₂ cup more water and cook for 30 to 40 minutes. Fluff the rice with a fork and let stand, covered, for 10 minutes. Let the rice cool slightly and then refrigerate for 30 minutes to 1 hour.

Meanwhile, in a large mixing bowl, combine the beans, scallions, tomatoes, cucumber, and garlic. Blend in all remaining ingredients. Fold in the chilled rice. Refrigerate for 1 to 2 hours before serving.

Makes 6 servings

Per Serving: 306 Calories; 10g Protein; 8g Fat; 50g Carbohydrates; 0mg Cholesterol; 811mg Sodium; 9g Fiber.

Heartland Barbecued Corn-on-the-Cob

6 to 8 ears of corn (do not shuck)
1 large pot of cold water
2 or 3 limes, quartered
Salt and freshly ground black pepper to taste

Preheat the grill until the coals are gray to white.

Soak the corn in the cold water for 30 minutes. Remove from the water, drain, and pat dry.

When the fire is ready, place the unshucked corn on the grill. Cook over moderate heat for 15 to 20 minutes, turning every 5 minutes or so. To determine the degree of doneness, peek at the corn and check the tenderness of the kernels.

When the corn is done, remove from the grill and allow to cool for a few minutes. Shuck off the husks and discard. (Be sure to remove any bits of corn silk.) Cut the cobs in half crosswise and rub some cut limes over the kernels. Pass the extra lime wedges at the table and allow guests to season with salt and pepper to taste. Serve with Louisiana Red Bean and Rice Salad and California Grilled Vegetable and Tofu Kebabs.

Makes *6* servings

Per Ear of Corn: 86 Calories; 3g Protein; 1g Fat; 20g Carbohydrates; 0mg Cholesterol; 13mg Sodium; 2g Fiber.

California Grilled Vegetable and Tofu Kebabs

¹/₂ pound extra-firm tofu, cubed
¹/₄ cup canola oil
¹/₄ cup red wine vinegar or balsamic vinegar
¹/₄ cup dry white wine
3 tablespoons vegetarian Worcestershire sauce (see Helpful Hint)
1 tablespoon Dijon mustard
1 tablespoon dried parsley
¹/₂ teaspoon salt

¹/₂ teaspoon freshly ground black pepper
2 medium zucchinis, sliced into ¹/₂-inch rounds
2 large yellow or green bell peppers, cut into 1-inch squares
12 ounces button mushrooms, woody stems removed
1 pint cherry tomatoes
2 small red onions, quartered and separated into pieces

Helpful Hint:

There are several brands of Worcestershire sauce on the market that do not contain anchovies. Check the labels of the brands in your super-market or natural food store to find a vegetarian version.

Preheat the oven to 375° F.

Place the tofu on a lightly greased baking pan and roast for 15 to 20 minutes, until lightly browned. Turn the cubes after about 10 minutes. Remove from the oven and let cool slightly. Set aside until ready to skewer the vegetables. (Roasting gives the tofu a "meaty" texture.)

Preheat the grill until the coals are gray to white.

Combine the oil, vinegar, wine, Worcestershire sauce, mustard, parsley, salt, and pepper in a medium mixing bowl. Set aside.

Thread the vegetables and tofu onto sixteen 10-inch barbecue skewers, alternating the vegetables and tofu for color. With a pastry brush, baste the skewered vegetables with the wine-mustard mixture, covering them completely and dabbing in between vegetables.

Place the skewers on a lightly oiled grill. Cook, basting occasionally, until the vegetables are tender but not charred, about 5 to 7 minutes on each side. Remove the finished kebabs to a warm platter and grill the remaining skewers. Serve the kebabs with the Louisiana Red Beans and Rice Salad, Heartland Barbecued Corn-on-the-Cob, and Southwestern Jícama Coleslaw.

Makes *16* kebabs

Per Kebab: 148 Calories; 5g Protein; 9g Fat; 15g Carbohydrates; 0mg Cholesterol; 269mg Sodium; 4g Fiber.

Southwestern Jícama Coleslaw

3 cups peeled, shredded jícama
   (see Helpful Hint)
3 cups shredded red cabbage
2 cups peeled, shredded carrots
1 cup low-fat or regular prepared
   coleslaw dressing

½ cup low-fat plain yogurt
2 tablespoons chopped fresh cilantro
½ teaspoon salt
½ teaspoon freshly ground black pepper

> **Helpful Hint:**
>
> Jícama, also called Mexican potato, is a tan-skinned, rotund, turnip-shaped tuber with a crisp, moist flesh and water chestnut flavor. Look for it in the specialty produce section of most supermarkets or in Mexican markets.

Combine all of the ingredients in a mixing bowl and blend thoroughly. Chill for at least 1 hour before serving.

Makes *6* servings

Per Serving: 204 Calories; 2g Protein; 14g Fat; 18g Carbohydrates; 1mg Cholesterol; 502mg Sodium; 3g Fiber.

Georgia Peach Tree Cobbler

6 ripe peaches, pitted and sliced
2 tablespoons dark rum
2 tablespoons fresh lime juice
½ teaspoon ground nutmeg
1 cup unbleached white flour
½ cup rolled oats (old-fashioned,
   not quick-cooking)
½ cup brown sugar

2 teaspoons baking powder
¼ teaspoon salt
3 tablespoons margarine or butter,
   softened
¾ cup buttermilk or 1% or 2% milk
¼ cup chopped pecans or slivered
   almonds (optional)
2 pints frozen low-fat yogurt

Preheat the oven to 375° F.

Combine the peaches, rum, lime juice, and nutmeg in a medium mixing bowl. Set aside for 10 minutes, mixing with a spoon after 5 minutes. Spoon the fruit into a lightly greased 9-inch round deep-dish baking pan or springform pan.

To make the topping, in a medium mixing bowl combine the flour, oats, brown sugar, baking powder, and salt. With a knife and fork or a pastry cutter, cut the margarine into the flour mixture until it resembles coarse meal. Stir in the buttermilk or milk and blend until batter is smooth.

Spread the batter evenly over the fruit. If desired, sprinkle the nuts over the top. Place the pan on the middle rack in the oven and bake until lightly browned on top, about 30 to 35 minutes. Remove from the oven and let cool for 30 minutes to 2 hours before serving.

Serve with a scoop of frozen yogurt on the side.

Makes *6* servings

Per Serving: 393 Calories; 10g Protein; 9g Fat; 71g Carbohydrates; 10mg Cholesterol; 402mg Sodium; 3g Fiber.

a Night of Fire and Spice

Habanero Salsa • Tortilla Chips • Black Bean–Chipotle Chili • West Indian Vegetable Curry • Coconut-Spinach Rice • Mint-Cucumber Raita • Mango Slush

recipes make 6 servings

Black Bean–Chipotle Chili (page 96) with tortilla chips and Coconut-Spinach Rice (page 97)

More and more people are cultivating a taste for hot and spicy food. Chile peppers exhilarate, electrify, and sear the palate with gustatory vigor. Fiery fare includes a wide spectrum of adventurous and ethnically diverse dishes from around the world. For those who share a passion for the piquant, a night devoted to the joys of *haute* hot cuisine is an epicurean pleasure, and a bonding experience as well.

This is the occasion to invite your adventurous friends. The meal begins with Habanero Salsa, a salsa spiked with the habanero chile, a curvaceous, colorful, and deceptively cute pod with a blistering heat. Fresh habanero chiles come in pale green, orange, and fire engine red and are often found in the specialty produce section of well-stocked supermarkets and Caribbean grocery stores. (Fiery Scotch bonnet peppers may be substituted or, to go a more moderate route, use a jalapeño or serrano pepper.)

The second course of Black Bean–Chipotle Chili exudes with a smoky, delectable nuance and a stick-to-your-ribs quality. Chipotle chiles are large jalapeño peppers that have been smoked and dried, intensifying their distinctive flavors.

The entrée—West Indian Vegetable Curry—offers a spicy refrain of hearty vegetables steeped in a West Indian curry sauce. The island curry is served with the aromatic Coconut-Spinach Rice, which soaks up a river of flavors. Mint-Cucumber Raita, a creamy yogurt condiment with Indian roots, soothes the palate between bites. The luscious Mango Slush is a cooling and welcome calm after the storm.

There are a few things to keep in mind before cooking with fresh chiles. When shopping, look for pods with smooth, taut skin and free of blemishes and wrinkles. To prepare a chile, cut the pod in half lengthwise, remove and discard the seeds, and finely chop the flesh. Removing the seeds (where much of the heat is concentrated) ensures a more equitable distribution of the fiery flavor.

If you have sensitive skin, it is a good idea to wear gloves; capsaicin, the heating element in chiles, may also irritate your skin. If your food is too spicy, a dairy product (such as yogurt or milk) should soothe your palate. (The dairy enzyme casein neutralizes the capsaicin.) However, if you are a true connoisseur of spicy cuisine, fan the flames and take another bite.

2 days to 2 hours before	Make the Black Bean–Chipotle Chili.
1 day before	Make the Mango Slush and freeze. Prepare the Habanero Salsa, cover, and store in the refrigerator.
6 to 8 hours before	Transfer the frozen Mango Slush to the refrigerator.
3 hours before	Make the Mint-Cucumber Raita and refrigerate.
1 to 1½ hours before	Make the West Indian Vegetable Curry.
30 minutes before	Make the Coconut-Spinach Rice.
Dinnertime	Transfer the Habanero Salsa to a serving bowl and place on the table with tortilla chips. Serve the Black Bean–Chipotle Chili as the first course. Arrange the West Indian Vegetable Curry, Coconut-Spinach Rice, and a small portion of Mint-Cucumber Raita on each dinner plate. Pass the extra raita at the table, along with bottles of hot sauce. Scoop out the Mango Slush after the plates are cleared.
What guests can bring	An acidic wine, such as gewürztraminer, goes well with spicy foods. Guests can also bring their favorite bottled hot sauce to pass around at the table. If anyone has a collection of chile pepper novelty items, this is the time to show them off.

Habanero Salsa

2 large tomatoes, diced
1 red or yellow bell pepper, seeded
    and diced
1 small red onion, diced
1 large clove garlic, minced
$\frac{1}{2}$ to 1 habanero or Scotch bonnet
    pepper, seeded and minced
2 tablespoons chopped fresh cilantro

Juice of 1 lime
$1\frac{1}{2}$ teaspoons dried oregano
1 teaspoon ground cumin
$\frac{1}{2}$ teaspoon salt
$\frac{1}{4}$ teaspoon cayenne pepper
One 16-ounce can crushed tomatoes
1 large bag flour tortilla chips

Combine all of the ingredients except the crushed tomatoes and chips in a
large bowl and mix well. Place three-quarters of the mixture in a blender
or a food processor fitted with a steel blade and process until mixture
becomes a chunky vegetable mash, about 5 to 10 seconds.

Return the mash to the bowl and blend in the crushed tomatoes. Cover
and chill for at least 1 hour, which will allow the flavors to develop. Stir
before serving. Serve with tortilla chips.

Makes about 5 cups

*Per $\frac{1}{4}$ Cup Without Chips: 16 Calories; 1g Protein; 0.1g Fat; 4g Carbohydrates;
0mg Cholesterol; 147mg Sodium; 0.6g Fiber.*

Black Bean–Chipotle Chili

1 tablespoon canola oil
1 large red onion, diced
1 large red or green bell pepper,
    seeded and diced
2 celery stalks, chopped
2 cloves garlic, minced
Two 15-ounce cans black beans, drained

One 8-ounce can stewed tomatoes
One 14-ounce can crushed tomatoes
1 or 2 canned chipotle peppers,
    seeded and minced
1 tablespoon chili powder
1 tablespoon dried oregano
$\frac{1}{2}$ teaspoon salt

In a large saucepan, heat the oil over medium-high heat. Add the onion,
bell pepper, celery, and garlic, and cook, stirring, for about 7 minutes.
Stir in all remaining ingredients, and cook for 30 minutes over low heat,
stirring occasionally.

Remove from the heat and let stand for 5 to 10 minutes before serving.

Makes 6 servings

*Per Serving: 296 Calories; 16g Protein; 4g Fat; 54g Carbohydrates; 0mg Cholesterol;
809mg Sodium; 17g Fiber.*

West Indian Vegetable Curry

1 tablespoon canola oil
2 medium tomatoes, diced
1 medium yellow onion, diced
1 small eggplant, diced
2 cloves garlic, minced
1 to 2 jalapeño or serrano chile peppers,
    seeded and minced
2 teaspoons minced fresh gingerroot
2 to 3 teaspoons curry powder

1¹/₂ teaspoons ground cumin
1 teaspoon salt
¹/₄ teaspoon ground turmeric
4 cups coarsely chopped, unpeeled white
    potatoes
2 large carrots, peeled and diced
3 cups hot water
One 15-ounce can chickpeas (garbanzo
    beans), drained (optional)

In a large saucepan, heat the oil over medium heat. Add the tomatoes, onion, eggplant, garlic, peppers, and ginger. Cook for 7 to 9 minutes, stirring occasionally. Stir in the curry powder, cumin, salt, and turmeric, and cook for 1 minute more.

Stir in the potatoes, carrots, and water and bring to a simmer. Cook over low heat, stirring occasionally, until the potatoes are tender, about 30 minutes.

To thicken, mash a few of the potatoes against the side of the pan with the back of a spoon. Stir in the chickpeas if desired and cook for 5 minutes more. Let stand for about 10 minutes before serving to allow flavors to develop.

Makes 6 servings

Per Serving: 125 Calories; 3g Protein; 3g Fat; 24g Carbohydrates; 0mg Cholesterol; 456mg Sodium; 4g Fiber.

Coconut-Spinach Rice

2 cups white basmati rice or long-grain
    rice (see Helpful Hint)
4 cups hot water
¹/₂ cup grated coconut, preferably
    unsweetened (see Helpful Hint)

10-ounce package frozen chopped
    spinach, thawed and drained,
    and squeezed dry
1¹/₂ tablespoons dried parsley
¹/₂ teaspoon salt
¹/₄ teaspoon cayenne pepper

Helpful Hint:

Basmati rice is a quick-cooking, long-grain, white or brown rice with a perfumey aroma. It's available in supermarkets, Asian groceries, and natural food stores.

In the photograph on page 92 the coconut was toasted before added to the dish for more flavor and color.

Combine all of the ingredients in saucepan and bring to a simmer. Cover the pan and cook over low heat until all of the water is absorbed, about 15 to 20 minutes. Remove from the heat and fluff with a fork. Let stand for 5 to 10 minutes before serving.

Makes 6 servings

Per Serving: 200 Calories; 5g Protein; 2g Fat; 40g Carbohydrates; 0mg Cholesterol; 231mg Sodium; 3g Fiber.

Mint-Cucumber Raita

16 ounces low-fat plain yogurt
1 medium cucumber, chopped (peeled if waxed)
2 or 3 tablespoons chopped fresh mint

Combine all of the ingredients in a mixing bowl. Cover and chill until ready to serve. Garnish with any remaining mint leaves.

Makes about 3 cups

Helpful Hint:
If fresh mint is unavailable, try using cilantro or basil for a different but still rewarding flavor.

Per ¼ Cup: 27 Calories; 2g Protein; 1g Fat; 3g Carbohydrates; 2mg Cholesterol; 27mg Sodium; 0.2g Fiber.

Mango Slush

1 cup apple juice
1 cup water
½ cup sugar
4 large ripe mangoes, peeled, pitted, and diced (see Helpful Hint)
Juice of 2 limes
1 small bunch fresh mint (optional)

Helpful Hint:
Mangoes are large kidney-shaped, oblong, or round fruits with a green and reddish-orange skin, coral flesh, and tropical flavor. Look for mangoes in the produce section of well-stocked grocery stores and Caribbean and Latin American markets. If you can't find mangoes, substitute about six fresh peaches.

Combine the juice, water, and sugar in a saucepan and bring to a simmer. Cook over low heat for about 10 minutes, stirring occasionally. Let cool slightly.

Add the mangoes, lime juice, and sugar liquid to a blender or a food processor fitted with a steel blade; purée. Transfer to a plastic container with a lid and freeze overnight.

About 8 hours before serving, transfer the frozen slush to the refrigerator. To serve, scoop the slush into small glass serving bowls. Garnish with fresh mint leaves.

Makes 6 servings

Per Serving: 112 Calories; 1g Protein; 0.4g Fat; 29g Carbohydrates; 0mg Cholesterol; 4mg Sodium; 3g Fiber.

Know Your Chiles

Here is a glimpse of some of the world's chile peppers. Many are available (on a seasonal basis) in the specialty section of well-stocked supermarkets and ethnic grocery stores.

Chipotle: This is a large jalapeño pepper that has been dried and smoked. Chipotles are available canned and ready to use, or dried and air-packed. (Soak the dried chiles for at least 30 minutes in warm water before using.) They have a smoky, piercing heat.

Jalapeño: This dark green (or red) thick-skinned pod is shaped like a bullet and has a medium heat level. Jalapeño chiles are one of the most versatile and widely available peppers.

New Mexico: This is a long, tapered green or red chile native to the American Southwest. The chile produces a dramatic, somewhat cherrylike heat and floral flavor. When dried, the chiles are often tied into holiday *ristra* wreaths.

Poblano: This is a large, forest green–purplish pod with a contorted anvil shape and sturdy skin. Poblanos have a raisiny flavor and medium heat. They are often roasted before using; a thin layer of skin is peeled off, leaving a smooth, tender flesh. Dried poblanos are called ancho chiles.

Red Fresno: These pods are similar to red jalapeños, only hotter. They have broad shoulders which taper to a point. Red Fresnos are interchangeable with jalapeños.

Serrano: This is a narrow, pointy pepper with a sharp, blistering heat that quickly fades. The pod is dense with seeds, which may account for its prickly heat. (A chile pepper's heat is concentrated near the seeds along the cell wall.)

Habanero and Scotch Bonnet: These very similar chiles are the world's hottest peppers. They are curvaceous, lantern-shaped pods with powerful, scorching, screeching heat and a floral flavor. The chiles can be orange, green, red, or yellow and are native to the Caribbean and South America. Handle with care.

an Italian
Garden
Party

Grilled Eggplant Antipasto with Basil • Tomato, Arugula, and Mozzarella Salad •

Pesto Garlic Bread • Bow-Tie Pasta Primavera • Strawberry-Lime Granita

recipes make 6 to 8 servings

Tomato, Arugula, and Mozzarella Salad (page 104) and Bow-Tie Pasta Primavera (page 106)

While Italian food is riding a wave of popularity, it is far more eclectic and sustaining than fancy faddish pasta or "gourmet" pizza. The real foundation and inspiration for authentic Italian cooking comes from the garden. Italian home gardens overflow with tomatoes, eggplant, zucchini, garlic, basil, and other earthly delights. Italians love to garden almost as much as they love to eat.

Even if you don't have a garden or have the time or desire to commune with soil and seedlings, it is easy to cultivate an Italian garden feast. For starters, a platter of Grilled Eggplant Antipasto with Basil sets the tone for the meal to come. The next course features a juicy Tomato, Arugula, and Mozzarella Salad, enhanced by the Italian leaf's delicate texture and peppery flavor.

The entrée is a colorful mélange of bow-tie pastas tossed with harvest vegetables and spritzed at the last minute with a mist of lemon for a hearty Bow-Tie Pasta Primavera. Warm Italian garlic bread smothered with pesto accompanies the pasta and fills the room with a distinctive herbal aroma. For dessert, there is a refreshing Strawberry-Lime Granita, a light and fruity ice confection.

This menu makes the most of advance preparation and minimizes time spent in the kitchen during the meal. In the Italian tradition, serve the courses in large serving platters at the table and allow guests to assemble their own plates family style. Parmesan or Romano cheese and a shaker of red pepper flakes should be passed at the table.

An Italian dinner theme is ideally suited for midsummer when a bumper crop of fresh herbs and vegetables comes to the market (or sprouts in your garden). It is also an opportunity to introduce your guests to the lighter side of Italian cooking and dispel the notion that Italian meals leave one feeling heavy and sluggish.

Kitchen Countdown

1 day before	Make the Grilled Eggplant Antipasto with Basil, cover, and refrigerate. Prepare the Strawberry-Lime Granita, cover, and store in the freezer.
3 to 4 hours before	Make the Tomato, Arugula, and Mozzarella Salad and refrigerate. Make the pesto for the Pesto Garlic Bread.
2 hours before	Move the frozen granita to the refrigerator.
30 to 45 minutes before	Cook the pasta and sauté the vegetables for the Bow-Tie Pasta Primavera.
15 minutes before	Prepare the Pesto Garlic Bread.
Dinnertime	Minutes before, assemble the dishes in large serving bowls and platters. Set the table with Parmesan or Romano cheese and red pepper flakes. Pass the dishes at the table and serve family style. For background music, play Luciano Pavarotti, or for more popular tastes, Frank Sinatra or Dean Martin.
What guests can bring	A bottle of red or white Italian wine completes the meal. Freshly ground coffee beans for after-dinner beverages are also nice.

Grilled Eggplant Antipasto with Basil

¹/₂ cup balsamic vinegar or quality red wine vinegar
¹/₂ cup fresh basil leaves, coarsely chopped
2 cloves garlic, minced
¹/₂ teaspoon salt
¹/₄ teaspoon red pepper flakes
2 large eggplants (about 2¹/₂ pounds total)
2 tablespoons olive oil

Preheat the grill until the coals are gray to white.

In a mixing bowl, combine the vinegar, basil, garlic, salt, and pepper flakes; set aside.

Cut the eggplants crosswise into ¹/₂-inch-thick slices. Place the slices on the grill and cook until tender and browned, about 5 to 7 minutes on each side. (Alternatively, broil the eggplant in the oven for the same amount of time.) Layer a large casserole dish with the eggplant slices and baste with the vinegar-basil dressing. Drizzle the oil over the top. Cover the dish and refrigerate for 4 hours or overnight.

Serve the eggplant as a light antipasto dish.

Makes 6 servings

> **Helpful Hint:**
> Balsamic vinegar is a premium well-aged, grape-based vinegar with a deep, smooth flavor and mild acidity.

Per Serving: 94 Calories; 2g Protein; 5g Fat; 13g Carbohydrates; 0mg Cholesterol; 184mg Sodium; 5g Fiber.

Tomato, Arugula, and Mozzarella Salad

6 large tomatoes, seeded and coarsely chopped
1 medium bunch arugula (about ¹/₃ pound), stems removed
1 medium red onion, chopped
¹/₂ pound part-skim mozzarella cheese, cubed, or to taste
2 or 3 cloves garlic, minced

3 tablespoons olive oil
2 tablespoons balsamic vinegar or red wine vinegar
¹/₄ cup chopped fresh parsley
1 teaspoon Dijon mustard
¹/₂ teaspoon salt
¹/₂ teaspoon freshly ground black pepper

> **Helpful Hint:**
> Arugula is a narrow green leaf with a spicy, herbal flavor. It is also known as rocket or roquette.

Toss all of the ingredients in a large salad bowl. Cover and refrigerate for 1 to 2 hours before serving.

Serve the salad over a bed of green leaf lettuce.

Makes 6 servings

Per Serving: 201 Calories; 11g Protein; 13g Fat; 11g Carbohydrates; 22mg Cholesterol; 393mg Sodium; 2g Fiber.

Pesto Garlic Bread

4 cloves garlic, coarsely chopped
1/3 cup pine nuts or diced walnuts
2 ripe plum tomatoes, diced
1 cup packed fresh basil leaves
1 cup packed and coarsely chopped
    fresh spinach

1/4 cup olive oil
1/4 teaspoon salt
1/3 to 1/2 cup grated Parmesan
    or Romano cheese
2 loaves Italian bread, unsliced
    (about 2 pounds)

Place all of the ingredients except the cheese and bread in a blender or a food processor fitted with a steel blade. Process until the mixture is puréed, about 10 to 15 seconds, stopping at least once to scrape the sides. Transfer to a medium-size mixing bowl and fold in the cheese. Refrigerate until ready to serve.

Preheat broiler. Cut the loaves of bread in half lengthwise. Spread the pesto liberally over the cut sides. Place the bread on a baking sheet and broil about 2 to 3 minutes. Keep the bread warm until ready to serve. Cut into thick slices before serving.

Makes about *20* **slices or** *6* **servings**

Per Slice: 171 Calories; 5g Protein; 6g Fat; 24g Carbohydrates; 1mg Cholesterol; 320mg Sodium; 2g Fiber.

Bow-Tie Pasta Primavera

1 pound bow-tie pasta (farfalle)
2 tablespoons olive oil
2 cloves garlic, minced
1 medium green zucchini, cut diagonally
    into $^{1}/_{2}$-inch slices
1 medium yellow summer squash,
    cut diagonally into $^{1}/_{2}$-inch slices
1 large red or green bell pepper,
    seeded and diced
10 to 12 white button mushrooms, sliced
8 large plum tomatoes, diced

1 large bunch broccoli, cut into florets
    and blanched
$^{1}/_{2}$ cup mixed chopped fresh herbs
    (such as basil and parsley)
2 teaspoons dried oregano
$^{1}/_{2}$ teaspoon salt
$^{1}/_{2}$ teaspoon freshly ground black pepper
$^{1}/_{2}$ to 1 cup grated Parmesan
    or Romano cheese
2 lemons, quartered

Cook pasta according to package directions until al dente, about 9 to 12 minutes; drain. Transfer to a large bowl and cover.

Heat the oil in a large skillet over medium heat. Add the garlic, zucchini, yellow squash, bell pepper, and mushrooms. Cook, stirring, for about 7 to 10 minutes. Add the tomatoes, broccoli, herbs, oregano, salt, and pepper, and cook for 8 to 10 minutes over medium-low heat.

In a large serving bowl, combine the vegetables with the cooked pasta and toss together. Blend in the cheese. Squeeze 2 or 3 wedges of lemon over the pasta and vegetables. Offer the remaining lemons at the table.

Makes 6 servings

Per Serving: 440 Calories; 19g Protein; 9g Fat; 76g Carbohydrates; 5mg Cholesterol; 721mg Sodium; 10g Fiber.

Strawberry-Lime Granita

1 cup apple juice or orange juice
1 cup water
³/₄ cup sugar
4 cups diced fresh strawberries (about 2 pints)
Juice of ¹/₂ lemon
2 limes, quartered

In a saucepan, combine the apple or orange juice, water, and sugar. Bring to a simmer and cook over medium heat for about 10 minutes, stirring occasionally. Set aside and let cool slightly.

Add the strawberries, lemon juice, and sugar liquid to a blender or a food processor fitted with a steel blade, and process until smooth, about 10 seconds. Transfer to a plastic container, cover, and freeze for about 4 hours.

Purée or mash with a spoon again for 10 to 15 seconds. Return to the freezer for 4 hours more or overnight.

Before serving, slightly thaw the strawberry ice in the refrigerator for 2 hours or at room temperature for 15 to 20 minutes. To serve, scoop the granita into small serving bowls and squeeze wedges of lime over the top.

Makes 6 servings

Per Serving: 146 Calories; 1g Protein; 0.4g Fat; 37g Carbohydrates; 0mg Cholesterol; 3mg Sodium; 2g Fiber.

Farmer's Market

Fiesta

Gourmet Greens with Champagne Vinaigrette • Herb Garden Gazpacho •

Harvest Vegetable Grill • Pasta with Kale and Garlic Greens Pesto •

Strawberry-Rhubarb Crumble Pie

recipes make *6* to *8* servings

Pasta with Kale and Garlic Greens Pesto (page 114) and Harvest Vegetable Grill (page 113)

For summer entertaining, look no farther than your local farmer's market. It's where the season's local bounty comes to glorious fruition. There is a familiar "green" scent in the air, crowds ebb and flow from stand to stand, and vegetables and fruits harvested at their peak make their way from the garden to the kitchen, from the grower to the table. It is an ongoing celebration of community resources, spirit, and cooperation.

The farmer's market is also a food-lover's paradise. The walkways are lined with exotica: yellow cherry tomatoes, chartreuse and burgundy-fringed lettuces, pungent chile peppers, garlic greens, orange beets, and baskets of zesty herbs. A menu culled from the local harvest abounds with exotic greens, verdant herbs, and seasonal produce picked at its prime.

This meal begins with Gourmet Greens with Champagne Vinaigrette—a colorful salad of greens and lettuces, such as spicy arugula, red-fringed oak leaf, purplish radicchio, and feathery mizuma. You can create your own blend of gourmet greens or buy it already mixed (usually sold as *mesclun*, French for "mixed field greens"). The second course from the market is the chilled soup du jour of summer, gazpacho. Herb Garden Gazpacho is a robust version enlivened with a plethora of garden herbs.

For the main course, there is the inviting sight and aroma of vegetables sizzling on the grill. Harvest Vegetable Grill is accompanied by pasta tossed with braised kale and coated with a fragrant pesto of garlic greens, nuts, tomatoes, and Parmesan cheese (Pasta with Kale and Garlic Greens Pesto). Garlic greens, the long green tops of garlic, have the texture of sturdy scallions and an aromatic, toned-down garlic flavor; they remind one that garlic is indeed an herb, not a vegetable. (If garlic greens are unavailable, substitute your favorite pesto in this recipe.)

For dessert, there is a delectable Strawberry-Rhubarb Crumble Pie made with the classic farmer's market pairing of freshly picked sweet strawberries and sour stalks of rhubarb. Strawberry and rhubarb go together like sugar and spice.

Kitchen Countdown

1 day before	Bake the Strawberry-Rhubarb Crumble Pie; cover and refrigerate.
3 to 4 hours before (and up to 1 day before)	Make the Herb Garden Gazpacho and the vinaigrette for the Gourmet Greens with Champagne Vinaigrette; cover and refrigerate separately. Make the pesto for the Pasta with Kale and Garlic Greens Pesto; store in an airtight container and refrigerate.
2 hours before	Rinse and toss the greens for the Gourmet Greens; crisp in the refrigerator until dinner. Take the pesto out of the refrigerator.
1 to 3 hours before	Grill the vegetables for the Harvest Vegetable Grill.
30 minutes to 1 hour before	Complete the Pasta with Kale and Garlic Greens Pesto.
15 minutes before	Toss the Gourmet Greens with the Champagne Vinaigrette.
Dinnertime	Arrange the serving bowls and platters on the table. Serve the Herb Garden Gazpacho as the first course, accompanied by loaves of market bread, followed by the salad, grilled vegetables, and pasta. If desired, offer frozen yogurt with the pie.
What guests can bring	A bouquet of flowers or whole-grain bread from the local market.

Gourmet Greens with Champagne Vinaigrette

1 large bunch red or green oak leaf lettuce, torn into large, bite-size pieces
1 large bunch frisée or mizuma, torn into large, bite-size pieces
1 medium bunch watercress or arugula, trimmed
½ pint red or yellow cherry tomatoes, halved
1½ to 2 cups shredded red cabbage (optional)
1 medium cucumber, sliced (peeled if waxed)
2 medium carrots, peeled and shredded
1 recipe Champagne Vinaigrette (recipe follows)

Combine all of the greens in a large salad bowl; toss together gently.
Arrange the remaining vegetables around the edge of the bowl in a decorative fashion. Chill until ready to serve.

Just before serving, drizzle with the Champagne Vinaigrette and toss.

Makes 6 servings

Helpful Hint:
Frisée and mizuma are feathery leafy greens with mild mustardlike flavor.

Champagne Vinaigrette

½ cup canola oil or olive oil
¼ cup champagne vinegar or white wine vinegar
1½ tablespoons balsamic vinegar
2 teaspoons Dijon mustard
2 teaspoons honey
2 teaspoons mixture of dried herbs (including oregano, basil,
*   parsley, and mint) or 2 tablespoons chopped fresh herbs*
¼ teaspoon salt
¼ teaspoon freshly ground black pepper

Combine all of the ingredients in a mixing bowl and whisk thoroughly.
(Or pour into a screw-top jar and shake vigorously.) Refrigerate at least
2 hours (preferably overnight) to allow the flavors to meld.

Drizzle over the salad just before serving and toss.

Makes about 1¾ cups

*Per Serving with 1 Tbs. Vinaigrette: 104 Calories; 4g Protein; 7g Fat;
11g Carbohydrates; 0mg Cholesterol; 71mg Sodium; 4g Fiber.*

Herb Garden Gazpacho

4 medium ripe tomatoes, diced
1 medium red onion, diced
1 large green or red bell pepper, seeded and diced
1 large cucumber, peeled and diced
2 or 3 cloves garlic, minced
1 cup mixed fresh herbs (such as parsley, basil, mint, and oregano), chopped
$^1/_2$ to 1 teaspoon hot pepper sauce

$^1/_2$ teaspoon ground cumin
$^1/_2$ teaspoon salt
$^1/_2$ teaspoon freshly ground black pepper
4 cups canned tomato juice or vegetable juice
Sprigs of herbs (such as parsley, basil, mint, oregano) for garnish
8 ounces low-fat plain yogurt

Combine all of the ingredients except the yogurt in a large mixing bowl and mix thoroughly. Transfer about three-quarters of the mixture to a blender or food processor fitted with a steel blade; process for 5 to 10 seconds. Return mixture to the mixing bowl and blend with the remaining vegetables. Refrigerate the gazpacho for at least 2 hours, preferably overnight.

Serve the gazpacho in chilled bowls and garnish with sprigs of herbs. Offer the yogurt on the side as a condiment.

Makes *6* servings

Per Serving: 98 Calories; 4g Protein; 1g Fat; 18g Carbohydrates; 2mg Cholesterol; 730mg Sodium; 2g Fiber.

Harvest Vegetable Grill

$^1/_2$ cup canola oil
Juice of 2 lemons
1 tablespoon dried parsley, or 2 tablespoons fresh
1 teaspoon paprika
$^1/_4$ teaspoon salt
$^1/_2$ teaspoon freshly ground black pepper
1 or 2 poblano chile peppers (optional)

4 medium red bell peppers, seeded and halved
2 medium red onions, peeled and quartered
1 large, long unpeeled eggplant (about 1$^1/_2$ pounds), cut diagonally into $^1/_2$-inch slices
1 large zucchini or yellow summer squash (about 1 pound), cut diagonally into $^1/_2$-inch slices

Preheat the grill until the coals are gray to white.

In a small mixing bowl, whisk together the oil, lemon juice, parsley, paprika, salt, and pepper. Place the peppers, onions, eggplant, and zucchini or squash in a large shallow dish or bowl. With a pastry brush, "paint" the vegetables with the dressing, coating all sides.

When the fire is ready, place the vegetables on the lightly oiled grill. Cook the vegetables until they become tender and develop grill marks, about 5 to 7 minutes on each side. Transfer them to a large mixing bowl as they become done.

(continues)

After the peppers have cooled slightly, cut them in half and discard the seeds. Using a butter knife or your hands, peel or rub off the blackened skin. Julienne the peppers and return to the mixing bowl. Dice the poblano chiles, if using. Toss all of the grilled vegetables with the remaining dressing.

Transfer to a large serving platter and serve alongside the Pasta with Kale and Garlic Greens Pesto, or refrigerate and serve as a cold dish.

Makes *6* servings

Per Serving: 115 Calories; 3g Protein; 5g Fat; 18g Carbohydrates; 0mg Cholesterol; 51mg Sodium; 6g Fiber.

Pasta with Kale and Garlic Greens Pesto

Pesto

2 cups chopped garlic greens
   (see Helpful Hint)
$^1/_2$ cup diced walnuts
2 medium tomatoes, diced
2 cups packed fresh basil leaves
$^1/_2$ cup extra virgin olive oil
$^1/_2$ teaspoon salt
$^1/_2$ teaspoon freshly ground black pepper
$^1/_2$ cup grated Parmesan or Romano
   cheese

Pasta

1 very large bunch kale or 2 medium
   bunches (about 2 pounds), rinsed,
   stems trimmed, and coarsely
   chopped
$^1/_4$ cup water
$1^1/_4$ pounds small ziti or pasta spirals

Helpful Hint:

If garlic greens are not available, substitute 1½ cups to 2 cups of your favorite pesto for the pesto recipe given above.

Combine all of the pesto ingredients except the cheese in a blender or a food processor fitted with a steel blade; purée. Transfer to a medium mixing bowl and fold in the cheese. Refrigerate until ready to serve.

In a large pot over medium heat, cook the kale in the water, stirring frequently, until wilted, about 5 minutes. Drain and set aside.

Cook pasta according to package instructions until al dente, about 9 to 11 minutes. Drain and cool under cold running water; drain again. Transfer to a large mixing bowl.

Add pesto and kale and toss. Transfer to a large serving bowl and serve immediately, or refrigerate and serve as a cold entrée. Pass extra Parmesan cheese at the table.

Makes *6* servings

Per Serving: 622 Calories; 20g Protein; 29g Fat; 77g Carbohydrates; 5mg Cholesterol; 751mg Sodium; 7g Fiber.

Strawberry-Rhubarb Crumble Pie

Crumble Topping

½ cup chopped walnuts
¼ cup brown sugar
9-inch frozen deep-dish pie shell, broken
*   into very small pieces*

Pie Filling

2 cups diced fresh rhubarb
*   (about 4 stalks)*
2 cups sliced fresh strawberries
*   (about 1½ pints)*
¾ cup brown sugar
¼ cup apple juice or orange juice
½ teaspoon ground nutmeg or cinnamon
2 tablespoons cornstarch

9-inch frozen deep-dish pie shell

Preheat the oven to 375° F.

To make the topping, in a small mixing bowl, blend together the nuts, sugar, and pie shell pieces, forming a streusel-like mixture. Set aside.

To make the filling, in a medium saucepan, combine the rhubarb, strawberries, sugar, juice, and nutmeg or cinnamon. Cook over low heat, stirring occasionally, until the mixture thickens, about 8 to 10 minutes. Remove from the heat and gradually whisk in the cornstarch. Set aside to cool for about 5 minutes.

Pour the fruit mixture into pie shell. Sprinkle the crumble topping evenly over the pie. Place on a baking pan and bake on the middle rack until the edges are light brown and the center is firm, about 45 minutes to 1 hour. Remove from the oven and let cool to room temperature. Refrigerate for 4 hours or overnight.

Makes *6* servings

Per Serving: 402 Calories; 4g Protein; 20g Fat; 55g Carbohydrates; 0mg Cholesterol; 279mg Sodium; 3g Fiber.

a Sizzling *Southwestern* Supper

Roasted Chile Guacamole • Winter Squash Pilaf •

Spinach-Vegetable Burritos • Spicy Black Beans •

Jícama-Tomato Salsa • Pumpkin Flan

recipes make *4* servings

Spinach-Vegetable Burritos (page 121) and Roasted Chile Guacamole (page 120) with tortilla chips

The cuisine of the American Southwest is a harmonious blend of Native American, Spanish, and Mexican cultures. The Southwestern pantry traditionally is filled with corn, beans, pumpkin, all kinds of squash, tortillas, herbs, and feisty chiles. The fare is brightly colored and flavored, easy to prepare, and unpretentious—perfect for casual entertaining.

The ideal time to serve a southwestern-inspired meal is from midsummer to late autumn, when many of the market staples are at their peak. The motif is a pleasurable divergence from the tried-and-true dinner routine, and this menu imparts an appreciation of one of America's authentic and most popular regional cuisines.

It's easy to be creative with this theme supper: Decorate with symbols and colors of the Southwest—scenes of desert flowers, cactus plants, adobe houses, linens in pink, mauve, and tan, a large basket of bright sweet and hot peppers as the centerpiece, and postcards of Georgia O'Keeffe paintings on the table settings.

Dinner begins with a rustic Roasted Chile Guacamole infused with roasted chile peppers. Every good guacamole hinges upon ripe, luscious avocados. (You can determine the degree of ripeness by gently pressing it with your thumb; it should give slightly.) Avocados will ripen in a few days at room temperature, so shop early if you have doubts about locating ripe "alligator pears," as they are sometimes called.

The centerpiece of this southwestern menu is Spinach-Vegetable Burritos—tortillas filled with a medley of colorful vegetables. The burritos are flanked by a trio of accompaniments: Winter Squash Pilaf, a rice dish studded with colorful pieces of butternut squash; Jícama-Tomato Salsa, a hearty, lime-scented salsa using the crisp, brown tuber called jícama, and a side of Spicy Black Beans. Pumpkin Flan seals the meal with a rich, creamy finale.

These recipes make four hefty dinners or six light meals. If you are serving six, offer a tossed green salad with the meal. For a soothing beverage, a robust Mexican beer will complement the spirited flavors.

Kitchen Countdown

3 or 4 days before	Purchase avocados. Store ripe avocados in the refrigerator and unripe avocados at room temperature.
1 day before	Prepare the crudités and Pumpkin Flan. Cover and store in the refrigerator.
3 to 4 hours before	Make the Roasted Chile Guacamole and Jícama-Tomato Salsa. Cover and store in the refrigerator.
1½ hours before	Chop the vegetables for the Winter Squash Pilaf.
1 hour before	Chop and sauté the vegetables for the Spinach-Vegetable Burritos. Cook the pilaf.
30 minutes before	Prepare the Spicy Black Beans.
15 minutes before	Set table with Roasted Chile Guacamole and tortilla chips and/or crudités.
Minutes before	Finish making the burritos.
Dinnertime	Serve the Roasted Chile Guacamole with tortilla chips and/or crudités as an appetizer. Arrange filled burritos on large, oval serving plates. Spoon Winter Squash Pilaf and Spicy Black Beans along sides of burritos. Serve the flan when all of the plates have been cleared.
What guests can bring	Flavored tortilla chips for the guacamole.

Roasted Chile Guacamole

2 or 3 poblano or red New Mexico chile
    peppers (see Helpful Hint)
1 small red bell pepper
2 ripe avocados, chopped
1 large tomato, diced
1/4 cup finely chopped red onion
2 cloves garlic, minced
2 tablespoons minced fresh cilantro
Juice of 1 lime
1/2 teaspoon ground cumin
1/2 teaspoon salt

Helpful Hint:

Poblano chiles are large, forest green pods shaped like an anvil. They have a raisinlike flavor and moderate heat. (Dried poblanos are called anchos.) New Mexico chiles are long, tapered, red or green pods with a fruity, addictive heat. (Red ones are slightly hotter.) If neither is available, mild Anaheim chiles may be used, but add a dash of hot sauce or minced jalapeño pepper to the guacamole to make up for lost heat.

Roast the chiles and bell pepper by placing over an open flame or beneath a broiler until the skin is charred, about 5 minutes per side. Remove from the heat and let cool for a few minutes. With a butter knife or your fingers, peel off the charred skin and discard. Remove the seeds and finely chop the remaining flesh. Set aside in a bowl.

Meanwhile, add the remaining ingredients to a large mixing bowl and mash together with a potato masher or fork, forming a chunky paste. Mash in the roasted chiles and bell pepper. Transfer to a serving bowl and refrigerate for 2 to 3 hours before serving. Serve with tortilla chips and/or crudités.

Makes about 4 cups

Per 1/4 Cup: 44 Calories; 4g Protein; 4g Fat; 4g Carbohydrates; 0mg Cholesterol; 72mg Sodium; 0.8g Fiber.

Winter Squash Pilaf

1 tablespoon canola oil
1 medium red onion, chopped
2 cloves garlic, minced
3 cups hot water
2 cups diced butternut squash or other
    winter squash
1 1/2 cups long-grain white rice, brown
    rice, or wehani rice (see Helpful
    Hint)
1/2 teaspoon salt
1/2 teaspoon freshly ground black pepper
3 or 4 tablespoons chopped fresh parsley

Helpful Hint:

Wehani rice is a mahogany-colored, aromatic rice available in natural food stores and some supermarkets.

In a medium saucepan, heat the oil over medium heat. Add the onion and garlic and cook, stirring, for 4 minutes. Stir in the water, squash, rice, salt, and pepper, and bring to a boil. Cover the pan and cook over low heat until all of the liquid is absorbed, about 15 to 20 minutes. (If using brown or wehani rice, add 1/4 cup more water and cook for 35 to 40 minutes.)

Fluff the rice and stir in the parsley. Let stand, covered, for 10 to 15 minutes before serving.

Makes 4 servings

Per Serving: 254 Calories; 5g Protein; 4g Fat; 51g Carbohydrates; 0mg Cholesterol; 273mg Sodium; 5g Fiber.

Spinach-Vegetable Burritos

2 teaspoons canola oil
1 medium zucchini, diced
12 to 14 white button mushrooms,
    sliced
1 large green or red bell pepper,
    seeded and diced

Two 10-ounce packages frozen chopped
    spinach, thawed, drained, and
    squeezed dry
1½ cups corn kernels, fresh or frozen
Four 10-inch flour tortillas
1 to 1½ cups shredded low-fat or regular
    Monterey Jack or Swiss cheese

In a large skillet, heat the oil. Add the zucchini, mushrooms, and bell pepper and sauté for 7 minutes. Stir in the spinach and corn. Cook for 5 to 10 minutes over medium heat, stirring occasionally. Keep warm until ready to fill the tortillas.

Warm the tortillas by steaming or placing them over high heat for a few seconds. Alternatively, wrap the tortillas in foil and place in warm oven (200° F) for about 5 minutes.

Blend the cheese into the vegetable mixture and reheat for about 1 minute. Spoon the vegetable and cheese mixture into the center of the tortillas, forming a log. Wrap the tortillas around the vegetable mixture and place seam-side down in the center of the individual serving plates. Spoon Winter Squash Pilaf (recipe follows) along one side of serving plate and Spicy Black Beans (below) along the other side. Garnish with Jícama-Tomato Salsa (page 122).

Makes 4 servings

Per Serving: 300 Calories; 11g Protein; 9g Fat; 38g Carbohydrates; 20mg Cholesterol; 292mg Sodium; 8g Fiber.

Spicy Black Beans

1 tablespoon canola oil
1 medium red onion, diced
2 cloves garlic, minced
1 or 2 serrano, jalapeño, or chipotle
    chiles, seeded and minced
One 15-ounce can black beans, drained

One 15-ounce can stewed tomatoes
1½ teaspoons dried oregano
1 teaspoon ground cumin
½ teaspoon salt
½ teaspoon freshly ground black pepper
2 to 4 tablespoons chopped fresh parsley

In a medium saucepan, heat the oil over medium heat. Add the onion, garlic, and chiles, and cook, stirring, for 4 minutes. Stir in the beans, tomatoes, oregano, cumin, salt, and pepper; cook for 7 to 10 minutes over low heat, stirring frequently. Stir in the parsley and cook for 2 or 3 minutes more. Remove from the heat and keep warm.

When ready to serve, spoon the beans alongside Spinach-Vegetable Burritos (see previous recipe).

Makes *4* servings

Per Serving: 221 Calories; 11g Protein; 4g Fat; 37g Carbohydrates; 0mg Cholesterol; 602mg Sodium; 12g Fiber.

Jícama-Tomato Salsa

2 ripe tomatoes, diced
1 cup peeled, diced jícama (see Helpful Hint)
⅓ cup chopped red onion
1 red Fresno or jalapeño pepper, seeded and minced
2 tablespoons chopped fresh cilantro
½ teaspoon salt
Juice of 1 lime

Combine all the ingredients in a medium mixing bowl. Refrigerate until ready to serve. Use to garnish Spinach-Vegetable Burritos (page 121).

Makes about *3* cups

Helpful Hint:

Jícama, also called Mexican potato, is a tan-skinned, rotund, turnip-shaped tuber with a crisp, moist flesh and water chestnut flavor. Look for it in the specialty produce section of most supermarkets or in Mexican markets.

Per ½ Cup: 24 Calories; 8g Protein; 0 Fat; 8g Carbohydrates; 0mg Cholesterol; 264mg Sodium; 0.8g Fiber

Pumpkin Flan

1 cup brown sugar
¹/₄ cup water
2 large eggs
2 large egg whites
1 cup skim or other low-fat milk

One 14-ounce can low-fat sweetened,
    condensed milk
One 16-ounce can pumpkin purée
¹/₄ teaspoon ground nutmeg
¹/₄ teaspoon ground cinnamon

Preheat the oven to 350° F.

Combine the sugar and water in a small sturdy saucepan. Cook over high heat for 1 minute. Do not stir. Reduce the heat to low and continue to cook without stirring until it becomes syrupy and turns amber, about 5 minutes. Pour equal amounts of the syrup into 8 medium ramekins and swirl to coat bottoms.

In a large mixing bowl, whisk together the eggs and egg whites. Beat in the milk, condensed milk, pumpkin, nutmeg, and cinnamon. Pour into the ramekins, filling each about three-quarters full. Set the ramekins into a large roasting pan. Fill the pan with hot water until it rises halfway up the sides of the ramekins. Place the pan in the oven and bake until the flans puff up slightly and are firm when gently jiggled, about 1 hour.

Remove from oven and cool to room temperature. Refrigerate for at least 4 hours, preferably overnight, before serving. Serve from the ramekins or run a knife blade between flan and ramekin and invert onto serving plate.

Makes *8* **servings**

Per Serving: 314 Calories; 8g Protein; 3g Fat; 64g Carbohydrates; 60mg Cholesterol; 221mg Sodium; 2g Fiber.

Caribbean

"Jump Up"

Barbecue

Tropical Salad with Mango Vinaigrette • Jamaican Jerk Vegetables •

Pumpkin Rice and Beans • Grilled Sweet Plantains • Calypso Fruit Bowl

recipes make 6 servings

Pumpkin Rice and Beans (page 129) and Calypso Fruit Bowl (page 131)

*I*n the Caribbean, a "jump up" barbecue is a festive outdoor party with friends, music, and food. On some islands, it is a weekly affair. The atmosphere is lively and spirited; food sizzles on the grill, rum punch flows, reggae music pulses, and dancing is inevitable. It is not an occasion to wear white gloves with pinkies raised.

The Caribbean is well known for sun-drenched beaches, turquoise waters, and carefree attitudes, but it also is a haven for adventurous cuisine. Island cooking is a kaleidoscope of sweet, spicy, herbal, and earthy tastes. Flavors from every corner of the world can be found simmering in the Caribbean kitchen. It is a true culinary melting pot.

This creative Caribbean menu promises light and healthful fare with bold tropical flavors. The menu begins innocently enough with Tropical Salad with Mango Vinaigrette, a tossed green salad dressed with a luscious dressing. This fruity palate cleanser is a prelude to the main attraction, and Jamaica's gift to the world's table—jerk barbecue; in this case, Jamaican Jerk Vegetables. Jerk is an authentic method of grilling or barbecuing over an open fire and is easily adapted to the vegetarian table. Jerk barbecue is sweet, spicy, herbal, and infused with a down-home appeal.

A signature flavor of jerk barbecue is provided by the Scotch bonnet pepper, the world's hottest chile. The Scotch bonnet pepper, native to the Caribbean, produces a scorching, searing heat and floral sensation; needless to say, it is best used in moderation and handled with care. Chile connoisseurs attest to its life-affirming properties; others may want to play it safe and substitute other, milder chiles. (See page 99 for tips on selecting and using chile peppers.)

Pumpkin Rice and Beans makes an inviting bed for the skewered jerk vegetables. In the Caribbean, West Indian pumpkin is consumed year-round and is often added to soups, stews, and rice dishes. It has a flavor and texture similar to butternut or Hubbard squash, both of which can be substituted if you can't find West Indian pumpkin in your market.

Another island staple, Grilled Sweet Plantains (also called banana vegetables or *plátanos*), rounds out the meal. Although plantains are typically fried, this more healthful, barbecued version "cooks" the plantains in their skins. For a light island dessert, try Calypso Fruit Bowl, a mélange of tropical fruits tossed with yogurt and served in hollowed-out pineapple shells.

So set the mood (and set the table) with colorful beach apparel, don your sunglasses, turn up the calypso or reggae music, and fire up the barbecue. Although you may be miles away from the tropics, you can still eat and indulge in the festival spirit of the Caribbean.

Kitchen Countdown

4 to 5 days before	Shop for plantains for the Grilled Sweet Plantains. If the plantains are green, store at room temperature for a few days to ripen.
1 day before	Prepare the marinade for the Jamaican Jerk Vegetables and the vinaigrette for the Tropical Salad with Mango Vinaigrette. Cover each and store in the refrigerator.
3 to 4 hours before	Skewer and marinate the jerk vegetables. Place in refrigerator.
2 to 4 hours before	Make the Calypso Fruit Bowl and refrigerate.
1 hour before	Finish the Tropical Salad with Mango Vinaigrette and refrigerate.
45 minutes before	Make the Pumpkin Rice and Beans.
15 to 30 minutes before	Grill the plantains.
10 minutes before	Grill the Jamaican Jerk Vegetables.
Dinnertime	Start with the Tropical Salad with Mango Vinaigrette. Serve the salad. Serve the Jamaican Jerk Vegetables, Pumpkin Rice and Beans, and Grilled Sweet Plantains on the same plate. After dinner, fill the pineapple shells with the tossed fruit for the Calypso Fruit Bowl.
What guests can bring	Calypso and reggae tapes or compact discs, Red Stripe beer, pictures of their island vacations, ingredients for piña coladas.

Tropical Salad with Mango Vinaigrette

Dressing

2 large ripe mangoes, peeled, pitted,
    and diced
1/3 cup apple cider vinegar
1/3 cup canola oil
1/3 cup apple juice or cider
1 to 2 tablespoons honey
1/4 teaspoon salt
1/4 teaspoon white pepper

Salad

1 medium head red leaf lettuce,
    coarsely chopped
1 medium head green leaf lettuce,
    coarsely chopped
2 large carrots, peeled and grated
1 medium cucumber, sliced (peeled if
    waxed)
1 small jícama, peeled and grated
2 ripe avocados, peeled, pitted, and sliced

To make the dressing, place all dressing ingredients in a blender or in a food processor fitted with a steel blade. Process until smooth, about 10 to 15 seconds. Serve at once or refrigerate for later. Makes about 2 1/2 cups.

To make the salad, in a large mixing bowl or wooden salad bowl, toss together the red and green leaf lettuces. Arrange the remaining ingredients along the perimeter. Refrigerate until ready to serve. Serve with mango dressing.

Makes *6* servings

Per Serving with 1 tablespoon Dressing: 183 Calories; 4g Protein; 13g Fat; 20g Carbohydrates; 0mg Cholesterol; 39mg Sodium; 5g Fiber.

Jamaican Jerk Vegetables

Marinade

8 large whole scallions, trimmed and
    coarsely chopped
2 medium yellow onions, diced
1/2 Scotch bonnet pepper or 1 large
    jalapeño pepper, seeded and minced
1 1/2 cups low-sodium or regular soy sauce
1 cup red wine vinegar
1/2 cup canola oil
1/3 cup brown sugar
1/4 cup chopped fresh parsley
1 1/2 teaspoons dried thyme
1 teaspoon nutmeg
1 teaspoon ground allspice or cinnamon

Vegetables

2 medium zucchinis, halved lengthwise
    and sliced into 1/2-inch-wide
    half-moons
2 large yellow or green bell peppers,
    seeded and cut into 1-inch squares
12 ounces button mushrooms, woody
    stems removed
1 pint cherry tomatoes

To make the marinade, place all the marinade ingredients in a blender or a food processor fitted with a steel blade. Process until puréed, about 10 seconds. Transfer to a container and refrigerate until ready to marinate the vegetables.

Thread the vegetables onto 10-inch barbecue skewers, alternating vegetables so they're attractive on the skewer. (Plan on 2 kebabs per guest.) Place the kebabs in a large casserole or baking dish, and pour the jerk sauce over all. Baste the vegetables, covering them completely with the marinade. Refrigerate for 2 to 4 hours, turning the kebabs after about 1 hour.

Preheat the grill until the coals are gray to white.

Remove the kebabs from the marinade and place on the lightly oiled grill; cook until the vegetables are tender but not charred, about 4 to 5 minutes on each side. Remove to a warm platter, and grill the remaining kebabs.

Serve the kebabs on a bed of Pumpkin Rice and Beans (recipe follows) accompanied by Grilled Sweet Plantains (page 130).

Makes *12* kebabs, *2* per serving

Per 2 Kebabs: 98 Calories; 5g Protein; 3g Fat; 16g Carbohydrates; 0mg Cholesterol; 412mg Sodium; 4g Fiber.

Pumpkin Rice and Beans

1 tablespoon canola oil
1 medium yellow onion, chopped
2 cloves garlic, minced
2 cups peeled, diced West Indian or sugar
  pie pumpkin or butternut or
  Hubbard squash (see Helpful Hint)
2 teaspoons curry powder

1/2 teaspoon salt
1/2 teaspoon freshly ground black pepper
3 cups water
1 cup low-fat or regular coconut milk
2 cups long-grain white rice
One 15-ounce can red kidney beans,
  drained

In a large saucepan, heat the oil over medium-high heat. Add the onion and garlic and cook, stirring, for 4 minutes. Stir in the pumpkin or squash, curry, salt, and pepper, and cook for 1 minute more.

Stir in the water, coconut milk, rice, and beans and bring to a simmer. Cover and cook over low heat for 15 to 20 minutes. Fluff the rice with a fork and remove from heat. Let stand, covered, for 10 to 15 minutes before serving.

Makes *6* servings

Helpful Hint:

West Indian pumpkin, also called *calabaza* or *calabasa*, is available in many Caribbean and Latin American markets. Butternut squash, Hubbard squash, or regular pumpkin may be substituted.

Per Serving: 301 Calories; 8g Protein; 5g Fat; 57g Carbohydrates; 0mg Cholesterol; 444mg Sodium; 7g Fiber.

Grilled Sweet Plantains

3 to 4 ripe yellow plantains (see Helpful Hint)
¼ teaspoon ground allspice or cinnamon

Helpful Hint

If the plantains are green and unripe, store at room temperature for about five days. Plantains will gradually ripen and turn yellow with black patches (like an over-ripe banana).

Preheat the grill until the coals are gray to white.

Cut off the tips of the plantains. Place the plantains on the lightly oiled grill and cook, turning once or twice, until the skin is charred and puffy, about 15 to 20 minutes. Take the plantains off the grill and let cool for a few minutes.

Cut and peel off the thick skin. Cut plantains in half lengthwise, then cut in half crosswise. Sprinkle with allspice or cinnamon, and transfer to serving plates. Serve with Jamaican Jerk Vegetables and Pumpkin Rice and Beans (previous recipes).

Makes 6 servings

Per Serving: 109 Calories; 1g Protein; 0.3g Fat; 29g Carbohydrates; 0mg Cholesterol; 4mg Sodium; 2g Fiber.

Calypso Fruit Bowl

1 medium pineapple
2 large ripe mangoes or papayas, peeled,
    pitted or seeded, and diced
2 ripe star fruit (carambola), cut cross-
    wise into ½-inch slices

3 or 4 kiwis, peeled and sliced
½ pint blueberries or raspberries
2 cups low-fat plain yogurt
1 tablespoon honey
¼ teaspoon nutmeg

Cut the pineapple in half lengthwise. (Do not cut off the crown.) Using a paring knife, cut a rectangle around the center core and remove. Scoop out the pulp, leaving the shell intact. Dice the pulp and place in a medium mixing bowl. Place the two pineapple shells in flat containers, cover, and place in the freezer for 2 to 4 hours.

Add the remaining ingredients to the diced pineapple and toss thoroughly. Refrigerate for 2 to 4 hours before serving.

To serve, place the partially frozen pineapple shells on serving platters and fill with the fruit-yogurt mixture.

Makes 6 servings

Per Serving: 172 Calories; 6g Protein; 2g Fat; 36g Carbohydrates; 5mg Cholesterol; 65mg Sodium; 5g Fiber.

a September Supper

Harvest

Golden Squash Bisque • **Roasted Garlic, Chickpea, and Basil Salad** • **Pumpkin-Vegetable Stew with Moroccan Spices** • **Couscous with Red Chard and Spinach** • **Green Tomato and Pear Chutney** • **Zucchini-Banana Bread with Roasted Sunflower Seeds**

recipes make *4* to *6* servings

Golden Squash Bisque (page 136) and Zucchini-Banana Bread
with Roasted Sunflower Seeds (page 139)

September is many things to many people. To some, it is back to school and an abrupt end of summer vacation. For others, it is the return to a normal work week and the demise of dress-down Fridays. September ushers in the football season and new fashions; outdoor concerts and afternoon picnics wind down. The spectacle of falling leaves replaces the smell of freshly cut grass; rakes replace gardening hoes. It is lights-out for summer.

To a cook or chef, September is a glorious month. The market beckons with big, beautiful squash of every shape and color, tomatoes both juicy red and tart green, prodigious zucchini, grandiose garlic, and baskets of fresh herbs. Leafy green vegetables, which are sparse and wilted in midsummer, triumphantly reappear in September. Most of all, the summer heat fades away, and it is enjoyable to be in the kitchen again.

This September harvest menu is perfect for a languid early autumn evening. It begins with a savory Golden Squash Bisque, a curry-scented soup glowing with warm autumnal flavors. Almost any winter squash or pumpkin can be used in this soup. Look for squash that are heavy and dense for their size. In general, heavier squash have thicker flesh and fewer seeds than lighter squash of the same size.

The main course features a Pumpkin-Vegetable Stew with Moroccan Spices, in this case, *harissa*, a Moroccan spice paste with hints of cumin, cayenne, and paprika. The hearty stew is accompanied by Roasted Garlic, Chickpea, and Basil Salad, an enticing marinated salad of roasted garlic, sweet cherry tomatoes, chickpeas, and brightly flavored basil. Roasting the whole garlic bulb brings out a mellow, but still endearingly potent, garlicky essence.

Couscous with Red Chard and Spinach, a combination of quick-cooking couscous and nutrient-rich leafy greens, makes another natural companion to the highly seasoned stew.

As the threat of frost approaches, green tomatoes are harvested before they are allowed to ripen on the vines. In the South, green tomato slices are often breaded and fried, but green tomatoes also make delightful condiments and sauces. They have a mildly sour flavor and firm texture. A Green Tomato and Pear Chutney, making use of the abundant unripe tomatoes available, cleanses the palate with sweet and tart sensations.

For an after-dinner treat that is delightful but not too sweet, there is Zucchini-Banana Bread with Roasted Sunflower Seeds, one zucchini creation you will never grow tired of.

Kitchen Countdown

1 to 2 days before	Make the Green Tomato and Pear Chutney and refrigerate.
4 hours before	Bake the Zucchini-Banana Bread with Roasted Sunflower Seeds.
2$\frac{1}{2}$ to 3 hours before	Roast the garlic for the Roasted Garlic, Chickpea, and Basil Salad.
2 hours before	Make the salad and marinate in the refrigerator.
1$\frac{1}{2}$ hours before	Make the Golden Squash Bisque.
1 hour before	Make the Pumpkin-Vegetable Stew with Moroccan Spices.
15 to 30 minutes before	Cook the Couscous with Red Chard and Spinach; take the chutney out of the refrigerator.
Dinnertime	Decorate the table with autumn gourds, winter squash, and dried flowers. Serve Golden Squash Bisque as the first course. Arrange the Roasted Garlic, Chickpea, and Basil Salad, Couscous with Red Chard and Spinach, and Pumpkin-Vegetable Stew with Moroccan Spices on large supper plates. Transfer Green Tomato and Pear Chutney to a serving bowl and pass at the table. Serve the Zucchini-Banana Bread with Roasted Sunflower Seeds for dessert, accompanied by hot beverages.
What guests can bring	Perhaps a fancy coffee or tea to accompany the Zucchini-Banana Bread.

Golden Squash Bisque

1 tablespoon canola oil
1 medium yellow onion, diced
2 stalks celery, sliced
2 medium tomatoes, diced
2 cloves garlic, minced
2 teaspoons minced fresh gingerroot
2 teaspoons curry powder
1 1/2 teaspoons ground cumin

1/4 teaspoon turmeric
1 teaspoon salt
1/8 to 1/4 teaspoon cayenne pepper
5 cups water or vegetable stock
4 cups peeled, diced butternut, Hubbard,
    or red kuri squash
1 large carrot, peeled and diced
1/4 cup chopped fresh parsley

In a large saucepan, heat the oil over medium-high heat. Add the onion and celery and cook, stirring, for about 4 minutes. Add the tomatoes, garlic, and ginger and cook, stirring, for 3 to 4 minutes more. Stir in the curry, cumin, turmeric, salt, and cayenne, and cook for 1 minute more over low heat, stirring frequently.

Add the water or vegetable stock, squash, and carrot, and cook over medium-low heat, stirring occasionally, until the squash is tender, about 25 minutes. Remove from the heat and let the soup cool slightly.

Transfer the mixture to a blender or food processor fitted with a steel blade and process until smooth, about 10 seconds. Pour into soup bowls and sprinkle the parsley over the top. Serve hot.

Makes 4 servings

Per Serving: 161 Calories; 4g Protein; 6g Fat; 29g Carbohydrates; 0mg Cholesterol; 570mg Sodium; 9g Fiber.

Roasted Garlic, Chickpea, and Basil Salad

1 medium head garlic
2 tablespoons olive oil
2 tablespoons balsamic vinegar
1 1/2 teaspoons Dijon mustard
1/4 teaspoon salt
1/2 teaspoon freshly ground black pepper

Two 15-ounce cans chickpeas (garbanzo
    beans), drained
24 cherry tomatoes, halved
12 to 14 leaves purple or green basil, cut
    chiffonade style (see Helpful Hint)
1 tablespoon chopped fresh chives

Helpful Hint:

To cut basil chiffonade style, stack basil leaves, and roll them lengthwise into a "cigar." Slice crosswise into very narrow strips.

Preheat the oven to 350° F.

Wrap the whole head of garlic in foil. Bake for about 30 minutes. Remove the garlic from the oven, unwrap, and let cool to room temperature. Peel off the skin from each of the cloves. Chop 4 to 6 cloves, or to taste; save any remaining cloves for another use.

In a large mixing bowl, whisk together the oil, vinegar, mustard, salt, and pepper. Stir in the chopped garlic, chickpeas, tomatoes, basil, and chives. Chill for 1 to 2 hours before serving.

Makes 4 servings

Per Serving: 331 Calories; 12g Protein; 7g Fat; 58g Carbohydrates; 0mg Cholesterol; 834mg Sodium; 12g Fiber.

Pumpkin-Vegetable Stew with Moroccan Spices

1 tablespoon canola oil or olive oil
1 medium yellow onion, diced
1 red bell pepper, seeded and diced
2 or 3 cloves garlic, minced
2 large ripe tomatoes, diced
1 ¹/₂ tablespoons harissa (see Helpful Hint)
3 cups water
4 cups peeled, diced sugar pie pumpkin or other winter squash
1 medium parsnip or turnip, peeled and diced
¹/₂ teaspoon salt
2 cups corn kernels, fresh or frozen

In a large saucepan heat the oil over medium-high heat. Add the onion, bell pepper, and garlic, and cook, stirring, for 4 minutes. Add the tomatoes and cook, stirring, for 2 minutes more. Add the harissa and cook, stirring, for 1 minute more. Stir in the water, pumpkin or squash, parsnip or turnip, and salt, and bring to a simmer. Cook over medium-low heat, uncovered, for about 15 minutes, stirring occasionally.

Stir in the corn and cook, stirring occasionally, until the squash and parsnip are tender, about 15 minutes more.

Let stand for 10 minutes before serving. To thicken, mash the squash against the side of the pan with the back of a spoon.

Serve as a main dish with the Couscous with Red Chard and Spinach (recipe follows) on the side.

Makes 4 servings

Helpful Hint:

Harissa is available in the specialty section of well-stocked supermarkets. If unavailable, try substituting 1 teaspoon *each* of ground cumin, coriander, and paprika, and ¹/₂ teaspoon cayenne pepper.

Per Serving: 187 Calories; 5g Protein; 4g Fat; 38g Carbohydrates; 0mg Cholesterol; 282mg Sodium; 7g Fiber.

Couscous with Red Chard and Spinach

1 tablespoon canola oil
1 small red onion, diced
4 cups coarsely chopped mixture of red chard and spinach
2 ³/₄ cups water
¹/₂ teaspoon salt
¹/₂ teaspoon freshly ground black pepper
2 cups couscous
2 or 3 tablespoons chopped fresh parsley
Juice of 1 large lemon

In a medium saucepan, heat the oil over medium heat. Add the onion and cook, stirring, for 3 minutes. Stir in the chard and spinach, water, salt, and pepper, and bring to a simmer. Cook, uncovered, over medium heat, for about 4 minutes, stirring occasionally.

Stir in the couscous, cover the pan, and turn off the heat. Let stand until couscous has absorbed liquid and is soft, about 10 to 15 minutes.

Fluff the couscous with a fork, and stir in the parsley and lemon juice. Serve on the side with Pumpkin-Vegetable Stew with Moroccan Spices (previous recipe).

Makes 4 servings

Per Serving: 322 Calories; 10g Protein; 4g Fat; 61g Carbohydrates; 0mg Cholesterol; 340mg Sodium; 5g Fiber.

Green Tomato and Pear Chutney

1 large yellow onion, diced
4 or 5 green tomatoes, diced
4 pears, diced
1 cup red wine vinegar
1 cup apple cider
1 cup raisins, dark or golden

¹/₂ cup brown sugar
3 or 4 cloves garlic, minced
1 teaspoon ground cumin
¹/₂ teaspoon salt
¹/₂ teaspoon freshly ground black pepper
¹/₄ teaspoon ground cloves

Combine all of the ingredients in a large, nonreactive saucepan. Cook over medium-low heat, uncovered, stirring occasionally, until the mixture is soft but still chunky, 45 minutes to 1 hour. Remove from the heat and let cool to room temperature. Chill until ready to serve. (Chutney will keep several weeks in the refrigerator in an airtight container.) Serve at room temperature with Pumpkin-Vegetable Stew with Moroccan Spices (page 137).

Makes about *4* **cups**

Per ¼ Cup: 90 Calories; 1g Protein; 0.3g Fat; 23g Carbohydrates; 0mg Cholesterol; 76mg Sodium; 3g Fiber.

Zucchini-Banana Bread with Roasted Sunflower Seeds

1 cup buttermilk, 1% milk, or rice milk
½ cup canola oil
1 cup brown sugar
1 large egg plus 1 egg white
2 cups mashed ripe bananas (about 4 bananas)
2 cups grated zucchini or yellow crookneck squash (about 2 to 3 medium)
1 cup roasted sunflower seeds
2 cups unbleached white flour
½ cup rolled oats (old-fashioned, not quick-cooking)
2½ teaspoons baking powder
1 teaspoon salt
1 teaspoon ground allspice
1 teaspoon ground nutmeg

Preheat the oven to 375° F.

In a medium mixing bowl, whisk together the milk, oil, sugar, egg, and egg white until fully incorporated. Fold in the bananas, zucchini or squash, and ¾ cup of the sunflower seeds.

In a separate bowl, mix together all of the remaining ingredients except the reserved sunflower seeds. Gently mix the dry ingredients into the wet batter. Spoon the batter into 2 lightly greased 9 × 5–inch loaf pans. Sprinkle the remaining sunflower seeds over the tops. Bake until a toothpick inserted in the center comes out clean, about 45 to 50 minutes.

Remove from the oven and let stand on a rack (still in loaf pans) for about 15 minutes before serving. To serve, gently remove loaves from the pans and slice.

Makes *2* **loaves, about** *12* **slices each**

Per Slice: 168 Calories; 3g Protein; 8g Fat; 21g Carbohydrates; 9mg Cholesterol; 158mg Sodium; 2g Fiber.

a *Middle Eastern Feast*

Baba Ghanoush • Minty Fava Bean and Bulgur Salad •

Vermicelli and Squash Pilaf • Green Peas in Tomato Sauce •

Chocolate Pistachio Halvah Cookies

recipes make *6* servings

Vermicelli and Squash Pilaf (page 145) and Minty Fava Bean and Bulgur Salad (page 144)

An authentic Middle Eastern meal is a feast for the senses. The cuisine invokes the scents of fragrant mint and parsley, nutty tahini, seductive garlic, and citrusy lemon. One-pot dishes are filled with wholesome bulgur, rice, legumes, and vegetables. Toasty wedges of pita bread are shared and passed at the table. Food and lively conversation dominate the room.

A Middle Eastern dinner begins with an appetizer, or *mezze*. (Hummus is a well-known example.) Another favorite offering is Baba Ghanoush, a roasted eggplant dip with a smoky, enticing flavor. The baba ghanoush is served with wedges of pita bread or a platter of cut-up carrots, celery, broccoli, and radishes. The appetizer is followed by a Minty Fava Bean and Bulgur Salad radiant with lemon and mint.

The Middle Eastern meal revolves around a hearty one-dish pilaf of grains, pastas, and vegetables. (Rice and vermicelli are often cooked together in the same pot.) This meatless Vermicelli and Squash Pilaf includes winter squash, chickpeas, rice, and thin strands of noodles. A traditional side dish of Green Peas in Tomato Sauce accompanies the pilaf and functions as both a side vegetable and a condiment on the Middle Eastern table.

Although rich desserts are rarely served after a Middle Eastern meal—wedges of fresh fruit and seasonal berries are more common—sweets do make appearances at festive occasions. While there is a time and a place for baklava, the famous Middle Eastern treat, it may be too syrupy and buttery for this menu. Instead, Chocolate Pistachio Halvah Cookies aptly fill the bill. These nutty confections are made from tahini (a sesame seed paste), cocoa, and pistachios, a favorite nut.

This whole meal can be served as a substantial midday course on the weekend or as a supper with a theme. It is a casual meal that does not require a lot of fussing, so serve it to good friends and family members who will spice up the meal with good conversation.

Kitchen Countdown

1 day before	Make the Baba Ghanoush and the Chocolate Pistachio Halvah Cookies.
2½ hours before	Make the Minty Fava Bean and Bulgur Salad.
1 hour before	Prepare the Vermicelli and Squash Pilaf.
30 minutes before	Cook the Green Peas in Tomato Sauce.
Dinnertime	As the appetizer, serve the Baba Ghanoush in an ornate bowl. Place the bowl on a large plate surrounded with wedges of pita bread and/or crudités. Follow the appetizer with salad plates (or bowls) of Minty Fava Bean and Bulgur Salad. Serve the Vermicelli and Squash Pilaf on round dinner plates; pass the Green Peas in Tomato Sauce at the table. For dessert, serve the Chocolate Pistachio Halvah Cookies with a hot beverage.
What guests can bring	Loaves of pita bread. It's also a Middle Eastern tradition to serve dessert with a strong, espresso-like coffee, so guests can bring a specialty coffee for an after-dinner beverage.

Baba Ghanoush

2 medium eggplants (about 2 pounds),
  cut in half lengthwise
1/4 cup plus 1 tablespoon tahini (sesame
  seed paste) (see Helpful Hint)
1/4 cup chopped fresh parsley
2 cloves garlic, minced
2 tablespoons chopped pimientos

1 teaspoon ground cumin
1/2 teaspoon salt
1/2 teaspoon freshly ground black pepper
Juice of 1 large lemon
6 small pita breads, warmed and cut in
  wedges, or crudités

Preheat the oven to 400°F.

Place the eggplant on a lightly greased baking pan. Bake until tender, about 20 to 25 minutes. (Alternatively, grill the eggplant until the skin chars and the flesh is tender, about 7 to 10 minutes on each side.) Remove from the heat and cool slightly.

Meanwhile, in a mixing bowl, combine the remaining ingredients (except the pita or crudités). Set aside until the eggplants are ready.

When the eggplants have cooled, scoop out the flesh and chop; discard the outer skin. Add the eggplant pulp to the tahini mixture and blend thoroughly. Mash the mixture with the back of a spoon. Refrigerate the dip until ready to serve.

Serve the dip with pita bread and/or crudités.

Makes 3 cups

Per Tablespoon: 32 Calories; 1g Protein; 1g Fat; 4g Carbohydrates; 0mg Cholesterol; 64mg Sodium; 1g Fiber.

Helpful Hint:
Tahini is a paste of ground sesame seeds. Look for it in supermarkets, Middle Eastern markets, and natural food stores. The variety made from roasted sesame seeds will be more flavorful than the type made from raw sesame seeds.

Minty Fava Bean and Bulgur Salad

1 cup bulgur (finely ground cracked
  wheat) (see Helpful Hint)
1 cup boiling water
Two 15-ounce cans small fava beans
  or black-eyed peas, drained
2 large tomatoes, diced
1 medium cucumber, chopped

2 large scallions, whole, or 1 small
  red onion, chopped
2 cloves garlic, minced
3 tablespoons olive oil
Juice of 2 lemons
1/4 cup chopped fresh mint leaves
1/2 teaspoon salt
1/2 teaspoon freshly ground black pepper

Combine the bulgur and water in a mixing bowl and let soak for 20 to 30 minutes.

Helpful Hint:

Bulgur is a form of wheat—specifically, wheat berries that have been steamed, dried, and crushed. The grain is available in coarse, medium, and fine textures. It can be found in natural food stores and in the grain section of well-stocked grocery stores.

Meanwhile, combine the remaining ingredients in another mixing bowl and toss together. When the bulgur has absorbed all of the water, fold it into the bean mixture. Chill for at least 1 hour or overnight before serving.

Serve the salad in a serving bowl lined with green leaf lettuce.

Makes 6 servings

Per Serving: 259 Calories; 12g Protein; 8g Fat; 40g Carbohydrates; 0mg Cholesterol; 829mg Sodium; 10g Fiber.

Vermicelli and Squash Pilaf

8 ounces uncooked vermicelli or angel-hair pasta
2 tablespoons canola oil
1 tablespoon olive oil
1 medium yellow onion, chopped
12 to 14 button mushrooms, sliced
4 1/2 cups hot water
4 cups peeled, diced butternut squash (about 1 medium squash)
1 1/2 cups parboiled rice or long-grain rice
1 teaspoon ground cumin
1/2 teaspoon ground turmeric
1 teaspoon salt
1/2 teaspoon freshly ground black pepper
One 15-ounce can chickpeas (garbanzo beans), drained

With your hands, break up the vermicelli into small pieces.

In a large, deep skillet, heat the canola oil over medium heat. Add the vermicelli and pan roast the noodles, stirring frequently, until noodles are golden brown, about 10 minutes. Meanwhile, in a large saucepan, heat the olive oil over medium-high heat. Add the onion and mushrooms. Cook, stirring, for about 7 minutes. Stir in the water, squash, rice, cumin, turmeric, salt, pepper, and roasted vermicelli, and bring to a simmer.

Stir in the chickpeas, cover, and cook over low heat until all of the liquid is absorbed, about 20 minutes.

Fluff the pilaf with a fork and let stand for 10 minutes before serving.

Makes 6 servings

Per Serving: 464 Calories; 12g Protein; 9g Fat; 86g Carbohydrates; 0mg Cholesterol; 601mg Sodium; 10g Fiber.

Green Peas in Tomato Sauce

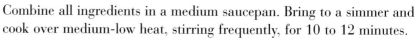

One 10-ounce package frozen green peas
One 15-ounce can tomato sauce
One 14-ounce can stewed tomatoes
2 teaspoons dried oregano
1 teaspoon ground cumin
$^1/_2$ teaspoon salt
$^1/_2$ teaspoon freshly ground black pepper

Combine all ingredients in a medium saucepan. Bring to a simmer and cook over medium-low heat, stirring frequently, for 10 to 12 minutes.

Remove from the heat and transfer to a serving bowl. Pass the peas and sauce at the table and serve on the side or over the top of the Vermicelli and Squash Pilaf (previous recipe).

Makes 6 servings

Per Serving: 80 Calories; 4g Protein; 0.4g Fat; 17g Carbohydrates; 0mg Cholesterol; 859mg Sodium; 5g Fiber.

Chocolate Pistachio Halvah Cookies

1 cup tahini (sesame seed paste)
³/₄ cup brown sugar
¹/₂ cup canola oil
¹/₄ cup 1% or 2% milk or soy milk
2 large eggs
2 cups unbleached white flour

¹/₂ cup coarsely chopped pistachios
   or sliced almonds
¹/₄ cup cocoa powder, sifted
1 teaspoon baking powder
¹/₂ teaspoon salt

Preheat the oven to 375°F. Line 1 or 2 cookie sheets with waxed paper.

In a medium mixing bowl or mixer, whisk together the tahini, sugar, oil, and milk or soy milk. Beat in the eggs one at a time.

In a separate bowl, mix together the remaining ingredients. Gently fold the dry ingredients into the wet ingredients.

Using an ice cream scooper or spoon, scoop the dough onto the cookie sheets. Bake until the edges are lightly browned, about 15 to 20 minutes. Cool on a rack for 10 minutes before serving or storing for later.

Makes about *1* dozen very large cookies

Per Cookie: 367 Calories; 9g Protein; 23g Fat; 34g Carbohydrates; 36mg Cholesterol; 164mg Sodium; 4g Fiber.

an Appetizing *Affair*

Homemade "Bread and Butter" Pickles • **Avocado and Gouda Quesadilla** •

Chickpea Skordalia • **Tofu Teriyaki Bites** • **Double Corn Polenta** •

Currant Citrus Scones

recipes make *6* servings

Tofu Teriyaki Bites (page 154), Double Corn Polenta (page 154),
and Chickpea Skordalia (page 153) with pita wedges

*T*here are times when entertaining does not require a formal or elaborate meal. It could be a casual gathering of friends before the theater or concert or after an early movie. Perhaps you wish to serve a spread of light bites for an afternoon tea or late night soiree, and you want to offer more than chips. This is the ideal time for appetizers, dips, and casual nibbles—small dishes designed to tweak one's appetite.

This globally inspired appetizer menu is perfect for almost any light entertaining occasion. The centerpiece is an Avocado and Gouda Quesadilla, a tortilla sandwich of sorts with a chunky filling of avocado, tomato, scallions, and smoky Gouda cheese. For embellishment, serve the quesadilla with Pico de Gallo (page 63) or your own favorite salsa.

The dip du jour is Chickpea Skordalia, a thick, luscious purée of potatoes, garlic, chickpeas, and more garlic. This version of skordalia, which is rooted in Greek cooking, makes a healthful alternative to the high-sodium and fat-drenched sour cream dips so prevalent on the cocktail party circuit. Accompany the Chickpea Skordalia with wedges of pita bread or crudités.

In keeping with the international theme, there are Tofu Teriyaki Bites, tasty tofu cubes that have been marinated in a soy, orange juice, and ginger marinade and roasted until crispy.

For easy consumption, the tofu cubes are speared with toothpicks. (What would an appetizer menu be without a platter of bite-sized treats impaled with toothpicks?)

For a taste of Americana, there are tangy Homemade "Bread and Butter" Pickles. These sweet, palate-whetting pickles are quick and easy to make and offer delicious proof that one does not have to undertake a full-scale canning operation to prepare scrumptious pickles at home. Commercial pickles have become so commonplace that it is a pleasant surprise whenever homemade pickles appear at the table.

From the Italian kitchen comes Double Corn Polenta, a dense cornmeal "cake" sated with corn, mozzarella cheese, and pimientos. The pie-shaped polenta has a mild flavor, soft texture, and is served in small wedges. Finally, with a nod toward the British penchant for afternoon tea, scones are offered as a light confection. These mildly sweet Currant Citrus Scones have an airy texture—not crumbly dry like so many scones tend to be. They make a perfect fit for this worldly menu of comforting flavors.

This "tasting" menu is ideally served as a casual buffet. You can offer your guests the formality of a dining room table or the relaxed comfort of living room couches and chairs, depending on your mood.

Kitchen Countdown

1 to 3 days before	Make the Homemade "Bread and Butter" Pickles, cover, and refrigerate.
2 to 4 hours before	Marinate the Tofu Teriyaki Bites in the refrigerator. Make the Currant Citrus Scones.
1 to 2 hours before	Make the Chickpea Skordalia.
1 hour before	Make the Double Corn Polenta.
30 to 45 minutes before	Make the Avocado and Gouda Quesadilla.
20 to 30 minutes before	Bake the Tofu Teriyaki Bites.
Dinnertime	Arrange all of the dishes on a buffet table. Set up a stack of "tasting plates" and invite guests to help themselves. Almost any beverage can be served: cocktails, tea, coffee, or daiquiris, depending on your needs and whims.
What guests can bring	Perhaps a variety of healthful snacks such as baked crackers and wedges of low-fat cheese.

Homemade "Bread and Butter" Pickles

4 medium pickling cucumbers,
*   cut crosswise into ¼-inch-wide slices*
1 small red bell pepper,
*   seeded and cut into rings*
1 small yellow bell pepper, seeded
*   and cut into rings*
1 medium yellow onion, sliced thin
3 ½ cups distilled white vinegar
1 ¼ cups sugar
2 tablespoons pickling spice
1 teaspoon salt
½ teaspoon turmeric

Combine all of the ingredients in a medium nonaluminum saucepan and bring to a simmer. Cook, uncovered, over medium heat for about 4 minutes, stirring occasionally. Remove from the heat and let cool to room temperature.

Transfer the pickle mixture to a food storage container, cover, and refrigerate for at least 24 hours, preferably for 2 or 3 days.

To serve, transfer the pickles and about half of the liquid to a serving bowl.

Makes about 4 cups or 6 servings

Per ¼ Cup: 22 Calories; 0.4g Protein; 0.1g Fat; 5g Carbohydrates; 0mg Cholesterol; 136mg Sodium; 1g Fiber.

Helpful Hint:

If desired, wrap the pickling spices in cheesecloth before simmering; remove before storing or serving.

If pickling spices are not available, make your own mixture, using 1 teaspoon *each* of the following: allspice berries, whole cloves, cumin seeds, black peppercorns, mustard seeds, crumbled bay leaves, and celery seeds.

Avocado and Gouda Quesadilla

2 medium tomatoes, diced
2 ripe avocados, peeled, pitted, and diced
2 large scallions (green and white parts),
*   chopped*
1 jalapeño pepper, seeded and minced
*   (optional)*
Juice of 1 lime

2 tablespoons minced fresh cilantro
½ teaspoon ground cumin
½ teaspoon salt
Four 9-inch flour tortillas
4 ounces shredded smoky Gouda
*   or provolone cheese*

Preheat the oven to 400°F.

In a medium mixing bowl, combine the tomatoes, avocados, scallions, jalapeño if desired, lime juice, cilantro, cumin, and salt.

Arrange 2 of the tortillas on a large baking pan. Spread an equal amount of the tomato-avocado mixture over the top of each tortilla. Sprinkle the cheese evenly over the top. Cover each tortilla with the remaining 2 tortillas.

Place the pan in the oven and bake until the tortillas are lightly browned and the cheese has melted, about 7 to 9 minutes. Remove from the oven. Using a wide spatula, transfer the quesadillas to warm serving plates. Cut each quesadilla into 6 wedges and serve hot.

Makes *12* **wedges or** *6* **servings**

Per Serving: 65 Calories; 2g Protein; 4g Fat; 4g Carbohydrates; 6mg Cholesterol; 117mg Sodium; 0.8g Fiber.

Chickpea Skordalia

6 cups water
2 cups peeled, chopped white potatoes
One 15-ounce can chickpeas (do not drain yet)
1/4 cup olive oil
2 teaspoons red wine vinegar
2 teaspoons lemon juice
4 cloves garlic, chopped
1/4 teaspoon salt
1/8 teaspoon cayenne pepper
Pita bread wedges and/or crudités

In a medium saucepan, bring the water to a boil. Add the potatoes to the boiling water and cook over medium-high heat until tender, about 15 to 20 minutes; drain.

Drain the chickpeas, reserving 1/2 cup of the liquid.

Add the chickpeas, reserved liquid, oil, vinegar, lemon juice, garlic, salt, and cayenne to a blender or food processor fitted with a steel blade and purée.

Add the potatoes and process until creamy, about 5 to 10 seconds more. Scrape the skordalia into a serving bowl and keep warm until ready to serve.

Serve with wedges of warm pita bread and/or crudités.

Makes about *2* **cups or** *6* **servings**

Per Tablespoon: 58 Calories; 2g Protein; 2g Fat; 9g Carbohydrates; 0mg Cholesterol; 97mg Sodium; 2g Fiber.

Tofu Teriyaki Bites

³/₄ cup orange juice
¹/₂ cup low-sodium or regular soy sauce
¹/₄ cup vegetarian Worcestershire sauce (see Helpful Hint)
¹/₄ cup plus 1 tablespoon brown sugar
1 tablespoon minced fresh gingerroot
2 tablespoons canola oil
¹/₂ teaspoon freshly ground black pepper
1 pound extra-firm tofu, cut into ³/₄-inch cubes

Helpful Hint:

There are several brands of Worcestershire sauce on the market that do not contain anchovies. Check the labels of the brands in your supermarket or natural food store to find a vegetarian version.

In a medium mixing bowl, whisk together all of the ingredients except the tofu. Add the tofu to the marinade. Cover the bowl and refrigerate for 2 to 4 hours. Stir the marinade after 1 hour.

Preheat the oven to 375°F. Line a 9 × 13–inch casserole or baking pan with aluminum foil.

With a slotted spoon or tongs, remove the tofu cubes from the marinade and arrange them in the casserole or on the pan. Bake until the tofu is firm and toasty brown, about 20 minutes. Remove the pan from the oven and let cool slightly.

Transfer the tofu cubes to a serving platter. Insert a frilly toothpick into each cube of tofu. Cover and keep warm until ready to serve.

Makes *6* servings

Per Serving: 88 Calories; 9g Protein; 2g Fat; 9g Carbohydrates; 0mg Cholesterol; 225mg Sodium; 0.7g Fiber.

Double Corn Polenta

2 ¹/₂ cups water
¹/₂ teaspoon salt
¹/₄ teaspoon freshly ground black pepper
1 cup fine yellow cornmeal
1 cup corn kernels, fresh or frozen
1 tablespoon chopped pimientos
¹/₂ to 1 cup grated mozzarella cheese

Combine the water, salt, and pepper in a heavy, medium saucepan and bring to a boil over high heat. Reduce the heat to low and slowly stir in the cornmeal with a wooden spoon. Continue stirring until no lumps remain. Stir in the corn and cook, uncovered, stirring frequently, until the mixture is thick, about 12 to 15 minutes. (A wooden spoon should be able to stand erect in the pot.)

Remove the pan from the heat and fold in the pimientos and cheese. Spread the polenta into a lightly greased 8- or 9-inch round deep-dish pie pan. Let cool to room temperature. Serve immediately or refrigerate for later. (To reheat the polenta, place in a 350°F oven for about 10 minutes.)

To serve, cut the polenta into wedges and arrange on a platter.

Makes 6 to 8 wedges or 6 servings

Per Serving: 98 Calories; 4g Protein; 1g Fat; 18g Carbohydrates; 4mg Cholesterol; 120mg Sodium; 3g Fiber.

Currant Citrus Scones

2 cups unbleached white flour
2 teaspoons baking powder
$^{1}/_{2}$ teaspoon salt
$^{1}/_{4}$ cup sugar
$^{1}/_{4}$ cup margarine or butter
2 large eggs, beaten
$^{1}/_{3}$ cup whole or low-fat milk
Zest of 1 orange or large lemon (about 2 teaspoons)
$^{1}/_{2}$ cup currants

Preheat the oven to 400°F. Lightly grease 1 large baking sheet.

In a medium mixing bowl, combine the flour, baking powder, salt, and sugar. With a pastry cutter or your fingers, blend the margarine or butter into the flour mixture until the texture resembles a coarse meal. Set aside.

In a separate small bowl, mix together the eggs, milk, and zest. Blend the egg mixture into the flour mixture, forming a moist dough. Fold in the currants.

With a spoon or melon ball scooper that holds about 2 tablespoons, scoop the dough onto the baking sheet. Gently form the dough into round balls; leave 2 to 3 inches between each ball. Bake until the scones are light brown, about 10 to 12 minutes. Remove from the heat and let cool to room temperature. Store in an airtight container until ready to serve.

Makes about 9 scones

Per Scone: 180 Calories; 5g Protein; 7g Fat; 26g Carbohydrates; 38mg Cholesterol; 230mg Sodium; 1g Fiber.

a

Native American

Thanksgiving

Red Bean Posole • Sweet Potato Succotash • Skillet Cornbread Dressing •

Baked Pumpkin Stuffed with Wild Rice Pilaf • Smothered Autumn Greens •

Cranberry-Maple Relish • Winter Squash–Pecan Pie

makes *8* servings

Baked Pumpkin Stuffed with Wild Rice Pilaf (page 161), Cranberry-Maple Relish (page 162), and Winter Squash–Pecan Pie (page 163)

*T*hanksgiving is a day when family and friends gather for a day of eating, watching football games and parades, eating, reminiscing, eating, giving thanks, and eating. More than any other holiday, Thanksgiving centers on the dinner table. Not surprisingly, the collective girth of the country probably expands by three belt notches.

This epicurean tradition began in 1621 when the Pilgrims joined the Native Americans at the supper table to commemorate their first harvest. According to lore, early Thanksgivings were resplendent with winter squash, pumpkin, corn, wild greens, and beans. Yes, there were wild turkey and game as well, but the air was filled with the spirit of the harvest.

With a little culinary ingenuity, it is possible to prepare a munificent and *meatless* Thanksgiving feast. This menu, inspired by the fare of Native American cuisine, is naturally healthful, vibrant, and, staying true to this hallowed rite of autumn, hearty and filling but not overwhelming. (You should be able to bend over and tie your shoes afterward.)

It begins with Red Bean Posole, a southwestern stew of hominy, vegetables, and herbs. Hominy is a dried form of corn; Indians dehydrated and preserved corn (similar to beans) and subsisted on the grains throughout the winter. In fact, the native American name for corn—maize—also is their word for life. Today, canned or frozen hominy can be found in well-stocked grocery stores.

A Native American feast would have to offer succotash, the indigenous pairing of corn and beans; we offer Sweet Potato Succotash. Historically, the two crops were grown in the fields together—the vines of pole beans climbed up the tall stalks of corn. Corn and beans were also harvested, preserved, and eaten together. Over time, the dish of succotash has come to include cream, butter, and even bacon, but this healthful version is fortified with nutrient-rich sweet potatoes, herbs, and spices.

What to serve as the Thanksgiving centerpiece is an annual quandary that legions of vegetarians encounter. For this menu, a splendid Baked Pumpkin Stuffed with Wild Rice Pilaf makes an impressive alternative to the big bird. Both pumpkin and wild rice are ancient staples dating from pre-Columbian America and form a natural alliance of flavors; pumpkin is subtle and sweet, wild rice earthy and grassy.

Crusty Skillet Cornbread Dressing gives the traditional Thanksgiving stuffing a new, more healthful identity. The dinner's condiment, Cranberry-Maple Relish, also has a new look and taste—both sweet and tart and heightened with maple syrup. It offers a vivid contrast to the lame, sticky-sweet canned relishes sold commercially. Easy-to-prepare Smothered Autumn Greens—greens braised in lemon juice—round out this holiday supper table.

For dessert, this Thanksgiving finishes with a flourish: a luscious winter squash pie studded with southern pecans. It is a fitting finale to an extraordinary feast.

Kitchen Countdown

2 to 3 days before	Make the Cranberry-Maple Relish and refrigerate; bake the cornbread for the Skillet Cornbread Dressing.
1 day before	Make the Winter Squash–Pecan Pie.
1 day to 1 hour before	Cook the Sweet Potato Succotash.
3 hours before	Decorate the table with Indian corn, colorful gourds, winter squash, and dried flowers.
2 hours before	Make the Red Bean Posole.
1½ hours before	Bake the pumpkin and make the pilaf for the Baked Pumpkin Stuffed with Wild Rice Pilaf.
30 to 45 minutes before	Cook the Smothered Autumn Greens. Make the Skillet Cornbread Dressing. Reheat the Sweet Potato Succotash. Bring Cranberry-Maple Relish to room temperature.
10 minutes before	Stuff the pumpkin with the Wild Rice Pilaf.
Dinnertime	Serve the Red Bean Posole as the first course. Serve the remaining dishes at the table family style, saving the Winter Squash–Pecan Pie for last.
What guests can bring	Frozen yogurt to go with the pie. Any interesting relishes they may have canned during the harvest season. A fall arrangement for the table centerpiece.

159

Red Bean Posole

1 tablespoon canola oil
1 medium yellow onion, diced
1 green bell pepper, seeded and diced
2 or 3 cloves garlic, minced
One 28-ounce can crushed tomatoes
One 15-ounce can red kidney beans, drained
One 15-ounce can hominy, drained
     (see Helpful Hint)

One 14-ounce can stewed tomatoes
2 to 3 tablespoons chopped fresh parsley
2 teaspoons chili powder
2 teaspoons dried oregano
$1/2$ teaspoon salt
$1/2$ teaspoon freshly ground black pepper

Helpful Hint:
You can find hominy either canned or frozen in most supermarkets.

In a large saucepan, heat the oil over medium heat. Add the onion, bell pepper, and garlic and cook, stirring, for about 5 minutes. Stir in all remaining ingredients, and cook for 20 to 25 minutes over medium-low heat, stirring occasionally.

Let stand for 5 to 10 minutes before serving. Ladle into bowls and serve hot.

Makes *8* servings

Per Serving: 160 Calories; 6g Protein; 3g Fat; 30g Carbohydrates; 0mg Cholesterol; 965mg Sodium; 7g Fiber.

Sweet Potato Succotash

1 large sweet potato (about 1 pound),
     diced (about 2 cups)
One 10-ounce package frozen
     baby lima beans
1 tablespoon canola oil
1 medium yellow onion, diced
1 red bell pepper, seeded and diced

2 cloves garlic, minced
2 cups corn kernels, fresh or frozen
2 tablespoons chopped fresh parsley
$1/2$ teaspoon dried thyme
$1/4$ teaspoon salt
$1/4$ teaspoon freshly ground black pepper

Place the sweet potato in a medium saucepan with boiling water to cover and cook until tender over medium heat, about 15 to 20 minutes; drain and set aside. Meanwhile, in another saucepan, place the lima beans in boiling water to cover and cook until tender over medium-high heat, about 10 minutes; drain and set aside.

In a large saucepan, heat the oil over medium heat. Add the onion, bell pepper, and garlic, and cook, stirring, for 5 minutes. Stir in the sweet potato, lima beans and all remaining ingredients, and cook for 5 to 7 minutes more over medium heat, stirring occasionally.

Transfer to a serving bowl.

Makes *8* servings

Per Serving: 195 Calories; 5g Protein; 3g Fat; 40g Carbohydrates; 0mg Cholesterol; 96mg Sodium; 6g Fiber.

Skillet Cornbread Dressing

1 recipe Cracked Pepper Cornbread
    (page 39) or other prepared
    cornbread
1 tablespoon canola oil
1 medium yellow onion, finely chopped

2 celery stalks, finely chopped
$1/2$ teaspoon ground sage
$1/4$ teaspoon salt
2 tablespoons chopped fresh parsley

Over a wide bowl, crumble the cornbread with your fingers, forming a coarse meal. Set aside.

In a large skillet, heat the oil over medium heat. Add the onion and celery and cook, stirring, for about 5 minutes. Stir in the crumbled cornbread, sage, salt, and parsley, and cook over low heat for 2 or 3 minutes, stirring frequently.

Transfer the dressing to a serving bowl and serve with Baked Pumpkin Stuffed with Wild Rice Pilaf and the rest of the Thanksgiving menu.

Makes about 6 cups

Per $3/4$ cup: 313 Calories; 7g Protein; 10g Fat; 38g Carbohydrates; 27mg Cholesterol; 446mg Sodium; 3g Fiber.

Baked Pumpkin Stuffed with Wild Rice Pilaf

Two 5- to 6-pound pumpkins
    or red kuri squash
1 tablespoon canola oil
1 medium yellow onion, diced
1 red or green bell pepper, seeded
    and diced
1 small zucchini, diced
2 cloves garlic, minced
$5 1/2$ cups water

2 cups long-grain brown rice
$1/2$ cup wild rice
$1 1/2$ tablespoons dried parsley
1 teaspoon salt
$1/2$ teaspoon freshly ground black pepper
$1/2$ teaspoon ground turmeric
1 cup green peas, fresh or frozen
$1/2$ cup grated Parmesan cheese (optional)

Preheat the oven to 375° F.

With a sharp knife, cut a 4- to 6-inch-wide lid off the top of each pumpkin. With a large spoon, scoop out the seeds and stringy fibers; discard or save for another use. Cover the holes in the top of each pumpkin with a square of foil large enough to keep the lid from falling back into the pumpkins, and set the pumpkin lids back on top. Place in a baking pan filled with about $1/2$ inch of water and bake until the insides are tender, about 50 minutes to 1 hour. Remove from the oven and keep warm.

Meanwhile, make the pilaf. In a large saucepan, heat the oil over medium-high heat. Add the onion, bell pepper, zucchini, and garlic, and cook, stirring, until the vegetables are tender, about 7 minutes. Stir in the water, brown rice and wild rice, parsley, salt, pepper, and turmeric, and bring to a simmer. Cover and cook over medium-low heat until all of the liquid is absorbed, about 45 minutes.

Fluff the pilaf with a fork, stir in the peas, and set aside for 5 to 10 minutes or until the pumpkins are ready. If desired, fold in the Parmesan cheese.

When the pumpkins are finished baking, discard the foil; spoon the pilaf into the pumpkins and cover with the lid.

Present the stuffed pumpkin on a large platter in the center of the table. When serving the pilaf, scrape the inside of the pumpkin so that each serving of rice also contains some cooked pumpkin.

Makes 8 servings

Per Serving: 255 Calories; 7g Protein; 3g Fat; 53g Carbohydrates; 0mg Cholesterol; 292mg Sodium; 9g Fiber.

Smothered Autumn Greens

1 medium bunch dandelion greens
1 medium bunch Swiss chard
2 teaspoon canola oil
1 medium yellow onion, finely chopped

3 or 4 cloves garlic, minced
Juice of 2 lemons
1 teaspoon salt
¹/₂ teaspoon freshly ground black pepper

Place the greens in a colander and rinse under cold running water. Remove the stems and coarsely chop the leaves.

Heat the oil in a skillet over medium heat and add the onion and garlic. Cook, stirring, for 2 to 3 minutes. Add the greens, lemon juice, salt, and pepper, and cook over low heat until the greens are wilted, about 2 minutes. Drain the excess liquid from the pan and place greens in a shallow serving platter. Cover until ready to serve.

Makes 8 servings

Per Serving: 27 Calories; 1g Protein; 0.8g Fat; 5g Carbohydrates; 0mg Cholesterol; 30Smg Sodium; 1g Fiber.

Cranberry-Maple Relish

12 ounces fresh or frozen cranberries
2 large apples or pears, diced
  (do not peel)
1 medium yellow onion, diced
³/₄ cup brown sugar
¹/₂ cup maple syrup

¹/₂ cup raisins
1¹/₄ cups red wine vinegar
1 cup apple juice or cider
¹/₂ teaspoon salt
¹/₂ teaspoon freshly ground black pepper
¹/₄ teaspoon ground cloves

Combine all of the ingredients in a large, nonreactive saucepan. Cook over low heat, stirring occasionally, until the mixture has a jamlike consistency, about 30 minutes.

Cool to room temperature before refrigerating. (It will keep several weeks in the refrigerator.) Serve at the Thanksgiving table.

Makes about *1* quart

Per ¹/₂ Cup: 200 Calories; 1g Protein; 0.3g Fat; 51g Carbohydrates; 0mg Cholesterol; 144mg Sodium; 4g Fiber.

Winter Squash–Pecan Pie

1 medium butternut squash or 2 cups cooked, mashed squash or canned pumpkin	*¹/₂ teaspoon salt*
	¹/₂ teaspoon nutmeg
	¹/₂ teaspoon cinnamon
1 cup low-fat, sweetened condensed milk	*¹/₄ teaspoon ground cloves*
1 large egg plus 1 large egg white, beaten	*One 9-inch graham cracker deep-dish pie crust*
1 cup chopped pecans	*2 pints low-fat frozen yogurt (optional)*
¹/₂ cup brown sugar	

Preheat the oven to 350° F.

Cut the squash in half lengthwise and scoop out the seeds and stringy fibers. Place the squash cut-side down in a baking pan filled with about ¹/₄ inch of water. Bake until the flesh is easily pierced with a fork, about 35 to 40 minutes. Remove from the oven, flip the squash over, drain, and let cool for a few minutes.

When the squash is cool, scoop out the flesh from the shells, and purée in a blender or mash by hand to a smooth pulp; measure out 2 packed cups. (Alternatively, use canned pumpkin.)

In a medium mixing bowl, blend together the cooked squash or pumpkin, condensed milk, beaten egg and egg white, ³/₄ cup of pecans, brown sugar, salt, nutmeg, cinnamon, and cloves. Pour the mixture into the pie crust and sprinkle the remaining pecans over the top. Place the pie in the oven and bake on the middle rack until a knife inserted into the center comes out clean, about 40 to 50 minutes.

Let the pie cool on a rack for several minutes before refrigerating. If desired, serve with frozen yogurt.

Makes *8* servings

Per Serving: 424 Calories; 7g Protein; 19g Fat; 59g Carbohydrates; 51mg Cholesterol; 358mg Sodium; 3g Fiber.

a New England *Christmas* Supper

Holiday Spinach Chowder • Cheddar-Vegetable Pot Pie • Boston Baked Beans with Seitan • Sautéed Zucchini with Tomatoes and Parsley • Cranberry-Orange Sauce • Apple-Berry Cake • Melon "Egg" Nog

recipes make *12* servings

Cheddar-Vegetable Pot Pie (page 168) and Cranberry-Orange Sauce (page 170)

*I*n New England, where a White Christmas is all but assured, the holiday is replete with joyous and festive sentiments of the season. Strains of the "The Nutcracker Suite" waft through stores and homes; village steeples chime with "Silver Bells." Wreaths hang from doorways and street lights; lights on freshly cut trees twinkle and blink in picture windows. It seems that all of New England is in a cheerful state of mind at Christmastime.

This holiday menu seeks to blend the healthy spirit of a New England Christmas with the new traditions of a vegetarian feast. It is a healthful supper intended for a large family gathering. The dinner begins with Holiday Spinach Chowder (or "chowdah"), the definitive New England soup of hearty vegetables and aromatic spices. Leafy spinach replaces the traditional seafood, and milk supplants heavy cream in this lighter, but just as flavorful, tureen.

Hearty and wholesome pot pies are another Yankee holiday tradition. This menu features Cheddar-Vegetable Pot Pie, a main dish oozing with warmth, comfort, and satisfying tastes. Accompanying the pot pie is another cherished regional staple, Boston Baked Beans. This rendition is sated with seitan, a high-protein wheat product with a meaty texture. A tasty mélange of Sautéed Zucchini with Tomatoes and Parsley fills out the plate. The abundance of Cape Cod cranberries inspires the brightly flavored Cranberry-Orange Sauce.

This enlightened Christmas dinner deserves a delectable, but not too heavy, dessert. Here is an opportunity to finally say no to Auntie's traditional two-ton fruitcake and discover instead a scrumptious Apple-Berry Cake, a light and refreshing creation filled with Vermont apples, Maine blueberries, and sweet spices.

This holiday menu also offers the chance to eschew traditional eggnogs, those rich libations loaded with egg yolks, cream, and sugar. Instead, indulge in a fruity, dairy-free Melon "Egg" Nog, the healthful alternative to the high-fat, supercaloric eggnogs of yore. So eat, drink, and be merry this Christmas!

Kitchen Countdown

2 days before	Make the Cranberry-Orange Sauce. Cover and refrigerate.
1 day before	Bake the Apple-Berry Cake; let cool to room temperature, cover, and refrigerate. Soak the beans overnight for the Boston Baked Beans with Seitan. Decorate the dining room with holiday wreaths, poinsettias, red and green candles, and other tasteful Christmas ornaments.
3 to 4 hours before	Cook the beans.
2 hours before	Make the Holiday Spinach Chowder. Finish making the baked beans.
1½ hours before	Make the Cheddar-Vegetable Pot Pie.
30 minutes before	Make the Sautéed Zucchini with Tomatoes and Parsley. Make the Melon "Egg" Nog.
Dinnertime	Serve the chowder as the first course. The baked beans, cranberry sauce, vegetable pot pie, and sautéed zucchini can be served family style at the table. After the plates are cleared, bring out the Apple-Berry Cake with hot beverages. The Melon "Egg" Nog can be served before or after the meal. Don't forget about the Christmas music.
What guests can bring	Presents, of course, and brown bread for the soup and Boston Baked Beans with Seitan would be nice. (It's traditional to mop up the baked beans with dark bread.)

Holiday Spinach Chowder

1 tablespoon canola oil
1 large yellow onion, diced
2 medium red bell peppers, seeded
    and diced
2 stalks celery, chopped
2 or 3 cloves garlic, minced
6 cups water or vegetable stock
4 cups peeled, diced white potatoes
    (about 4 medium potatoes)

2 tablespoons dried parsley
2 teaspoons dried oregano
2 teaspoons dried thyme
1 teaspoon salt
1 teaspoon freshly ground black pepper
10-ounce bag fresh spinach, rinsed,
    trimmed, and coarsely chopped
    (about 8 cups)
2 cups whole milk

In a large saucepan, heat the oil over medium-high heat. Add the onion, bell peppers, celery, and garlic, and cook, stirring, for 5 to 7 minutes. Add the water or stock, potatoes, parsley, oregano, thyme, salt, and pepper, and bring to a simmer. Cook over medium-low heat, stirring occasionally, until the potatoes are tender, about 20 to 25 minutes.

Stir in the spinach and return to a simmer; cook for 5 to 10 minutes more, stirring occasionally. Stir in the milk and return to a gentle simmer. Remove from the heat and let stand for 10 minutes.

To thicken, mash the potatoes against the side of the pan with the back of a spoon. Ladle the soup into bowls and serve hot.

Makes *12* servings

Per Serving: 128 Calories; 4g Protein; 3g Fat; 22g Carbohydrates; 6mg Cholesterol; 243mg Sodium; 4g Fiber.

Cheddar-Vegetable Pot Pie

Filling

1 tablespoon canola oil
1 large yellow onion, diced
2 cloves garlic, minced
2 cups water
2 medium parsnips, peeled
    and diced (about 1/2 pound)
2 cups diced white potatoes
    (peeled if desired)
4 medium carrots, peeled and diced
1 tablespoon dried parsley

1 teaspoon salt
1/2 teaspoon freshly ground black pepper
1 1/2 cups green peas, fresh or frozen
1 cup shredded low-fat cheddar cheese

Crust

4 cups unbleached white flour
    (see Helpful Hint)
1 1/2 teaspoons salt
1 1/2 cups canola oil
1/2 cup water

Preheat the oven to 400° F.

To make the filling, in a large saucepan heat 1 tablespoon of the oil over medium heat. Add the onion and garlic and cook, stirring, for 5 minutes. Add the water, parsnips, potatoes, carrots, parsley, salt, and pepper,

Helpful Hint:
You may substitute up to half of the unbleached white flour with whole-wheat pastry flour if you prefer.

and bring to a simmer. Cook over medium-low heat, stirring occasionally, until the vegetables are tender, about 20 to 25 minutes. Stir in the peas and cook for 5 minutes more. To thicken, mash the potatoes and parsnips against the side of the pan with the back of a spoon. Remove from the heat and let cool slightly.

To make the crust, in a large mixing bowl combine the flour and salt. Blend in 1½ cups of the oil and water and form a large moist ball of dough. Divide the dough into four balls of equal size.

On a lightly floured, flat surface, roll out the balls of dough into ⅛-inch-thick rounds about 10 inches in diameter. Place two of the rounds into the bottom of two lightly greased 9-inch round deep-dish pie pans. Bake for 5 to 7 minutes; cool for about 5 minutes.

Pour the filling equally into the pie pans. Sprinkle the cheddar cheese evenly over the tops. Cover the filling with the two remaining round crusts, and crimp the edges with a fork. Pierce the tops with a fork 2 or 3 times.

Bake until the tops are lightly browned, about 20 to 25 minutes. Cool for 10 minutes before serving. To serve, cut the pie into wedges and serve with the Boston Baked Beans with Seitan (page 170) and Sautéed Zucchini with Tomatoes and Parsley (next recipe).

Makes *12* servings

Per Serving: 466 Calories; 9g Protein; 27g Fat; 45g Carbohydrates; 6mg Cholesterol; 642mg Sodium; 4g Fiber.

Sautéed Zucchini with Tomatoes and Parsley

2 tablespoons olive oil	1½ teaspoons dried thyme
2 medium zucchini, cut into ½-inch slices	1 teaspoon salt
2 medium yellow squash, cut into ½-inch slices	½ teaspoon freshly ground black pepper
	One 14-ounce can stewed tomatoes
1 large red onion, sliced thin	¼ cup chopped fresh parsley

In 1 large or 2 medium skillets, heat the oil over medium heat. Add the zucchini, yellow squash, onion, thyme, salt, and pepper, and cook, stirring, for about 7 minutes. Stir in the tomatoes and parsley and simmer for 7 to 10 minutes more over medium heat, stirring occasionally. Cover the pan and keep warm until ready to serve.

Transfer to a warm serving platter and serve family style.

Makes *12* servings

Per Serving: 49 Calories; 0.9g Protein; 2g Fat; 6g Carbohydrates; 0mg Cholesterol; 186mg Sodium; 2g Fiber.

Boston Baked Beans with Seitan

1½ cups dried navy beans, soaked
    overnight and drained
1 tablespoon canola oil
1 medium yellow onion, diced
2 cloves garlic, minced
⅔ cup catsup

⅓ cup molasses
¼ cup brown sugar
3 tablespoons vegetarian Worcestershire
    sauce (see Helpful Hint)
½ teaspoon salt
⅓ pound seitan, diced (see Helpful Hint)

Helpful Hint:

There are several brands of Worcestershire sauce on the market that do not contain anchovies. Check the labels of the brands in your supermarket or natural food store to find a vegetarian version.

Helpful Hint:

Seitan is a food made from wheat gluten and has a meat-like texture. It is sold in natural food stores in the refrigerated section and as a mix on the shelf.

Place beans in a large saucepan and add water to cover. Bring to a simmer and cook over medium-low heat uncovered until tender, about 1 to 1½ hours. Drain the beans, discarding the liquid.

Preheat the oven to 350° F.

In a large flame-proof casserole or Dutch oven, heat the oil over medium heat. Add the onion and garlic and cook, stirring, for 4 minutes. Stir in the catsup, molasses, brown sugar, Worcestershire sauce, and salt, and cook over low heat, stirring frequently, for 3 to 4 minutes. Stir in the beans and seitan.

Cover the casserole and transfer to the oven. Bake for 40 to 50 minutes, stirring occasionally. Remove from the heat and keep warm until ready to serve.

Makes *12* servings

Per Serving: 212 Calories; 7g Protein; 2g Fat; 41g Carbohydrates; 0mg Cholesterol; 193mg Sodium; 6g Fiber.

Cranberry-Orange Sauce

4 cups cranberries (about 1 pound), fresh or frozen and thawed
Juice of 2 oranges
½ cup water
1 cup sugar
2 teaspoons orange zest

Combine the cranberries, orange juice, and water in a blender or a food processor fitted with a steel blade and process until thick and jamlike, about 5 to 7 seconds. Transfer to a medium mixing bowl and blend in the sugar and orange zest. Cover and refrigerate for at least 4 hours (preferably 1 to 2 days) before serving.

Makes *12* servings

Per Serving: 80 Calories; 0.2g Protein; 0.1g Fat; 20g Carbohydrates; 0mg Cholesterol; 0.7mg Sodium; 1g Fiber.

Apple-Berry Cake

½ cup orange juice
½ cup canola oil
1 cup granulated sugar
1 cup brown sugar
2 large eggs
2 teaspoons vanilla extract
4 cups diced red apples (about 6 medium) such as Cortland or Ida Red

1½ cups blueberries (fresh or frozen and thawed)
3 cups unbleached white flour
1 tablespoon baking powder
1 teaspoon salt
1 teaspoon nutmeg
1 teaspoon cinnamon
1 cup diced walnuts or pecans

Preheat the oven to 350° F.

In a large mixing bowl, blend together the orange juice, oil, and sugars until fully incorporated. Beat in the eggs and vanilla until creamy. Fold in the apples and berries.

In a separate medium mixing bowl, combine the flour, baking powder, salt, nutmeg, and cinnamon. Fold the dry mixture into the wet batter. Fold in the nuts.

Pour the batter into 2 lightly greased 9-inch round cake pans or springform pans. Place pans on the middle rack of the oven and bake until a toothpick inserted in the center comes out clean, about 50 to 55 minutes. Set on a rack to cool for 30 minutes to 1 hour. If desired, ice cake with Yogurt Cream Cheese Topping (see page 8). Cover and refrigerate until ready to serve.

Makes *12* servings

Per Serving with Frosting: 445 Calories; 7g Protein; 11g Fat; 86g Carbohydrates; 130mg Cholesterol; 327mg Sodium; 4g Fiber.

Melon "Egg" Nog

4 cups diced cantaloupe (about 1 medium)
2 large bananas, peeled and chopped
4 cups chilled rice milk or vanilla soy milk

¼ cup dark rum (optional)
2 tablespoons honey
2 teaspoons vanilla extract
2 teaspoons nutmeg

Combine all of the ingredients except the nutmeg in a blender and blend until creamy, about 10 seconds. Pour into a pitcher and keep chilled until ready to serve. To serve, pour the mixture into glasses and sprinkle the nutmeg over the top.

Makes *12* servings

Per Serving: 129 Calories; 3g Protein; 3g Fat; 23g Carbohydrates; 0mg Cholesterol; 63mg Sodium; 1g Fiber.

a _Kwaanza_ Feast

Black-Eyed Pea and Roasted Squash Salad • Jolof Party Rice •

Creole-Spiced Sweet Potatoes • Roasted Yellow Plantains •

Carrot-Corn Muffins • Jamaican Rum Cake

recipes make _6_ to _8_ servings

Jolof Party Rice (page 176) and Carrot-Corn Muffins (page 178)

Kwaanza is the celebration of African-American culture, heritage, and principles. It is a wholesome, family-oriented ritual combining diverse elements of African music, storytelling, dance, symbolism, and food. Kwaanza meals include dishes from wherever an African legacy can be felt, from Jamaica to West Africa, Brazil to the American South, and points elsewhere in the vast African diaspora.

Kwaanza is commemorated during the last week of the year and culminates on December 31 with a lavish feast called *karamu*. During the week of Kwaanza (which means "first fruits of the harvest" in Swahili), families discuss one of the Seven Principles (*Nguzo Saba*) every evening over dinner. The principles invoke discussions about character-building virtues such as unity, self-determination, collective work and responsibility, cooperative economics, purpose, creativity, and faith.

The creative spirit of Kwaanza can be felt throughout this vegetarian karamu. The first course is a southern-inspired Black-Eyed Pea and Roasted Squash Salad. In the American South, it is said that eating black-eyed peas on New Year's Eve will bring good fortune for the coming year.

The meal's centerpiece is Jolof Party Rice, a festive one-pot jambalaya-style dish traditionally served at celebrations and large gatherings throughout West Africa. Curry, ginger, and thyme give this meatless version of jolof rice an aromatic nuance and colorful amber presence.

Jolof Party Rice is served with Roasted Yellow Plantains, a staple enjoyed in both African and Caribbean cultures. Roasted Yellow Plantains have a sweet bananalike flavor and are a traditional Caribbean side dish. To ripen green plantains, store them at room temperature for four to five days. They should gradually turn yellow and develop dark spots (like an overripe banana).

Joining the plantains on the plate are Creole-Spiced Sweet Potatoes, a variation of Louisiana candied yams. Molasses endows these roasted sweet potatoes with a husky, sweet flavor and is nicely balanced by the piquant Creole seasonings.

Carrot-Corn Muffins are lighter and moister than most versions, and are made even lighter with beta carotene–rich carrots. Serve them in a basket to pass at the table.

For dessert, there is Jamaican Rum Cake, a dense confection laden with rum-soaked dried fruit and scented with island spices. This version is lighter than the traditional holiday rum cake (also called black cake), but just as satisfying, and it can be made well ahead of time.

Kitchen Countdown

4 or 5 days before	Shop for yellowish-green plantains. Store the plantains at room temperature.
1 to 2 days before	Bake the Jamaican Rum Cake.
3 to 4 hours before (and up to 1 day before)	Prepare the Black-Eyed Pea and Roasted Squash Salad and refrigerate.
2 to 4 hours before	Bake the Carrot-Corn Muffins.
1 to 1½ hours before	Make the Jolof Party Rice. Roast the sweet potatoes and plantains.
Dinnertime	Decorate the table with a red, green, and black patterned African kinte cloth. Serve Black-Eyed Pea and Roasted Squash Salad, Jolof Party Rice, and Creole-Spiced Sweet Potatoes family style at the table. Place the Carrot-Corn Muffins in a bread basket and pass during the meal. After dinner, serve the Jamaican Rum Cake with Jamaican Blue Mountain coffee.
What guests can bring	The symbolic props for Kwaanza, such as corn (symbolizing children), harvest vegetables (for crops), unity cups, Kwaanza candles, books, and heritage symbols (symbolizing gifts). Jamaican Blue Mountain coffee would be appropriate after dinner.

Black-Eyed Pea and Roasted Squash Salad

1 butternut or buttercup squash, halved lengthwise and seeded
3 tablespoons canola oil
2 tablespoons red wine vinegar
1¹/₂ teaspoons Dijon mustard
¹/₄ cup chopped fresh parsley or 2 tablespoons dried
¹/₂ teaspoon salt
¹/₂ teaspoon freshly ground black pepper
Two 15-ounce cans black-eyed peas, drained, or more if desired
4 scallions, whole, trimmed and finely chopped
2 large stalks celery, chopped
Lettuce leaves

Preheat the oven to 375°F.

Place the squash cut-side down in a baking pan filled with about ¹/₄ inch water. Bake until the squash is tender, about 30 to 40 minutes. Remove from the oven and let cool slightly. Scoop out the flesh and coarsely chop.

Meanwhile, in a large mixing bowl, whisk together the oil, vinegar, mustard, parsley, salt, and pepper. Fold in the squash, black-eyed peas, scallions, and celery. Chill for at least 2 hours before serving.

Serve the salad in a large bowl lined with lettuce.

Makes 6 servings

Per Serving: 221 Calories; 8g Protein; 8g Fat; 32g Carbohydrates; 0mg Cholesterol; 652mg Sodium; 8g Fiber.

Jolof Party Rice

1 tablespoon canola oil
1 medium yellow onion, finely chopped
1 large green or red bell pepper,
*   seeded and diced*
1 medium eggplant, diced
1 tablespoon minced fresh gingerroot
One 14-ounce can stewed tomatoes
2 to 3 teaspoons curry powder
2 teaspoons dried thyme leaves

1 teaspoon salt
¹/₂ teaspoon freshly ground black pepper
4 cups water or vegetable stock
2 cups long-grain white rice or
*   basmati rice*
3 or 4 carrots, peeled and diced
2 cups coarsely chopped and packed kale
*   or spinach*
2 tablespoons tomato paste

In a large saucepan, heat the oil. Add the onion, bell pepper, eggplant, and ginger, and cook over medium heat, stirring occasionally, about 8 to 10 minutes.

Add the tomatoes, curry powder, thyme, salt, and pepper, and cook for 1 to 2 minutes more. Stir in the water or stock, rice, carrots, kale or spinach, and tomato paste, and bring to a simmer. Cover and cook over low heat until all of the liquid has been absorbed, about 15 to 20 minutes. Fluff with a fork and let stand for 10 minutes before serving.

Makes *6* servings

Per Serving: 259 Calories; 6g Protein; 3g Fat; 54g Carbohydrates; 0mg Cholesterol; 1,104mg Sodium; 6g Fiber.

Creole-Spiced Sweet Potatoes

4 medium sweet potatoes, scrubbed and coarsely chopped
1/4 cup canola oil
1/4 cup dark molasses
2 tablespoons brown sugar
2 teaspoons dried thyme
1/2 teaspoon salt
1/2 teaspoon freshly ground black pepper
1/4 teaspoon white pepper
1/4 teaspoon cayenne pepper
1/4 cup chopped fresh parsley

Preheat the oven to 375°F.

In a large mixing bowl, toss together all of the ingredients except the parsley, coating the sweet potatoes completely. Place the sweet potatoes in a lightly greased casserole dish or baking pan and roast in the oven until tender, about 35 to 40 minutes. Stir the sweet potatoes after about 20 minutes.

Remove from the oven and let cool slightly before serving. To serve, place the sweet potatoes on a platter and sprinkle the parsley over the top.

Makes *6* servings

Per Serving: 257 Calories; 6g Protein; 7g Fat; 48g Carbohydrates; 0mg Cholesterol; 200mg Sodium; 4g Fiber.

Roasted Yellow Plantains

3 large yellow plantains
¼ teaspoon ground nutmeg, allspice, or cinnamon

Preheat the oven to 400°F.

Cut off the tips from the plantains. Place the plantains on a baking sheet and bake until the skin is charred and puffy, about 15 to 20 minutes. Remove the plantains from the oven and let cool for a few minutes.

Slice all the way through the plantains down the center lengthwise and peel away the skin. Cut the plantains in half crosswise, sprinkle with nutmeg, allspice, or cinnamon, and transfer to serving plates. Keep warm until ready to serve.

Makes 6 servings

Per Serving: 110 Calories; 1g Protein; 0 Fat; 29g Carbohydrates; 0mg Cholesterol; 4mg Sodium; 2g Fiber.

Carrot-Corn Muffins

1 cup yellow cornmeal
1 cup unbleached white flour
½ cup sugar
1 tablespoon baking powder
½ teaspoon salt

1 large egg plus 1 large egg white
1 cup buttermilk or soy milk
¼ cup canola oil
1 cup shredded carrots

Preheat the oven to 375°F.

Combine the cornmeal, flour, sugar, baking powder, and salt in a mixing bowl. In a separate bowl, whisk together the egg and egg white, buttermilk or soy milk, and oil. Gently fold the liquid ingredients into the dry ingredients until a batter is formed. Fold in the carrots.

Pour the batter into a lightly greased muffin pan. Bake until a toothpick inserted in the center comes out clean, about 20 minutes. Remove muffins from muffin pan and cool on a rack. To serve, place muffins in a basket and pass at the table.

Makes 12 muffins

Per Serving: 167 Calories; 3g Protein; 6g Fat; 26g Carbohydrates; 18mg Cholesterol; 245mg Sodium; 1g Fiber.

Jamaican Rum Cake

2 cups mixed chopped dried apricots,
    pitted dates, and raisins
1 cup dark rum
1/2 cup dark beer
1/2 cup canola oil
1/2 cup brown sugar
1/2 cup molasses

2 large eggs plus 1 large egg white
1 teaspoon vanilla extract
1 teaspoon ground nutmeg
1/2 teaspoon ground allspice
1 cup unbleached white flour
1 teaspoon baking powder
1/2 teaspoon salt

In a small mixing bowl, combine the dried fruit, rum, and beer. Set aside
for 4 hours or overnight at room temperature.

Preheat the oven to 350°F.

Place the fruit mixture in a blender or food processor fitted with a steel
blade and process to a pulp, about 5 to 10 seconds; set aside.

In another mixing bowl, blend together the oil, brown sugar, and
molasses. Beat in the eggs and egg white one at a time. Mix in the vanilla,
nutmeg, and allspice.

In a separate bowl, combine the flour, baking powder, and salt. Gently
fold the fruit pulp and the dry ingredients into the wet batter. Pour the
batter into a lightly greased, 9-inch round springform pan or cake pan.
Bake until a toothpick inserted in the center comes out clean, about
45 minutes to 1 hour.

Remove the cake from the oven and cool on a rack. Cover until ready
to serve. This cake can be made 2 or 3 days ahead of time.

Makes 8 **servings**

*Per Serving: 503 Calories; 5g Protein; 25g Fat; 69g Carbohydrates; 69mg Cholesterol;
241mg Sodium; 6g Fiber.*

Après-Ski

Dinner

Party

Split Pea, Mushroom, and Wild Rice Soup • **Quinoa, Broccoli, and Squash Casserole** •

Thyme-Roasted Sunchokes • **Sweet Potato–Zucchini Muffins**

recipes make ***6*** *servings*

Split Pea, Mushroom, and Wild Rice Soup (page 184)
and Sweet Potato–Zucchini Muffins (page 186)

*T*o some snow buffs, *après-ski* means heading to the nearest ski lodge and knocking down a few cold beers as quickly as possible. To others, it is a time for rest, recuperation, and replenishment. After a day on the slopes or ice-skating, bobsledding, or any other outdoor winter activity, the proper and welcome therapy is a home-cooked, down-to-earth meal.

Ski season is also soup season. This menu calls for a steaming bowl of Split Pea, Mushroom, and Wild Rice Soup, a healthful tureen of nourishing legumes, woodsy mushrooms, and nutty-tasting wild rice. The soup can be made a day in advance and reheated—the flavors actually improve with age.

On the heels of the soup course comes Quinoa, Broccoli, and Squash Casserole, a robust, straight-from-the-hearth meal sated with energy-boosting grains and hardy vegetables. Satisfying one's appetite should not be a problem here.

The casserole is served with a side of Thyme-Roasted Sunchokes, better known as Jerusalem artichokes—quite a misnomer, considering they are neither artichokes nor are they from Jerusalem. Sunchokes are gnarly root vegetables indigenous to North America and get their name from their sunflower relatives. Roasted sunchokes have a mildly nutty flavor and potatolike texture, and aptly balance the quinoa casserole.

Wholesome homemade Sweet Potato–Zucchini Muffins complete this casual midwinter meal. Serve these sweet and savory muffins with piping hot chocolate or mulled cider.

Although entertaining in winter can be a challenge—it is difficult to find some kinds of vegetables (for example, tomatoes)—it does not have to be daunting. There usually is a good supply of pantry staples and winter crops to choose from, such as grains, beans, pastas, winter squash, potatoes, and hardy leafy green vegetables. Planning a menu with do-ahead dishes is also a strategic objective.

So when it is brisk and chilly outside, this wholesome wintry menu will warm you up on the inside. And if, after conquering mountains and moguls your spirits still need a lift, sneak a little liqueur or brandy into the cider and cozy up next to the nearest fireplace after dinner. Bottoms up!

Kitchen Countdown

1 day before	Make the Sweet Potato–Zucchini Muffins. Let cool on a rack for 30 minutes, cover, and store overnight at room temperature.
2 $\frac{1}{2}$ hours before (or 1 day before)	Make the Split Pea, Mushroom, and Wild Rice Soup.
1 $\frac{1}{2}$ hours before	Bake the Thyme-Roasted Sunchokes.
1 to 1 $\frac{1}{2}$ hours before	Make the Quinoa, Broccoli, and Squash Casserole.
Dinnertime	Serve the Split Pea, Mushroom, and Wild Rice Soup as the first course. Serve the Quinoa, Broccoli, and Squash Casserole and Thyme-Roasted Sunchokes together on dinner plates. Offer Sweet Potato–Zucchini Muffins for dessert with the hot after-dinner beverages.
After the meal	Make a hot beverage, such as hot chocolate or mulled cider.
What guests can bring	A flavored liqueur to perk up the hot chocolate, or mulling spices for the cider.

Split Pea, Mushroom, and Wild Rice Soup

1 tablespoon canola oil
1 large red onion, diced
2 stalks celery, chopped
12 ounces button mushrooms, sliced
2 to 3 cloves garlic, minced
10 cups water
1 cup yellow or green split peas, rinsed
2 large carrots, peeled and diced

2 cups diced white potatoes (about
   2 medium), peeled if desired
1/2 cup wild rice (see Helpful Hint)
2 tablespoons dried parsley
2 teaspoons dried oregano
1 teaspoon freshly ground black pepper
1 teaspoon salt
Soup crackers

In a large saucepan, heat the oil over medium-high heat. Add the onion, celery, mushrooms, and garlic, and cook for about 7 minutes, stirring frequently.

   Stir in the water, split peas, carrots, potatoes, wild rice, parsley, oregano, and pepper, and bring to a simmer. Cook over medium-low heat, stirring occasionally, until the split peas are tender, about 1 1/2 to 2 hours.

   Stir in the salt and cook over low heat for 5 to 10 minutes more. Remove from the heat and let stand for 10 to 15 minutes before serving. Ladle the soup into bowls and serve with soup crackers.

Makes *6* servings

Helpful Hint:
Wild rice, a dark earthy grain with a grassy flavor, is available in the grain section of natural food stores and well-stocked supermarkets.

Per Serving: 245 Calories; 12g Protein; 3g Fat; 45g Carbohydrates; 0mg Cholesterol; 383mg Sodium; 12g Fiber.

Quinoa, Broccoli, and Squash Casserole

Helpful Hint:
Quinoa, pronounced "keen-wa," is an ancient grain native to South America. It is a tiny, ring-like grain with a nutty flavor and is a solid source of protein. Rinse quinoa thoroughly to remove a natural, bitter-tasting resin that coats the grains. Look for the grain in natural food stores and well-stocked grocery stores.

1 tablespoon canola oil
1 medium yellow onion, diced
1 red bell pepper, seeded and diced
1 medium zucchini, diced
2 cloves garlic, minced
4 1/2 cups hot water
2 cups quinoa, rinsed and drained
   (see Helpful Hint)
2 cups peeled, diced butternut squash
   (see Helpful Hint)

1/4 cup chopped fresh parsley or 2 tablespoons dried
1 teaspoon salt
1 teaspoon freshly ground black pepper
1 medium bunch broccoli (about
   1 pound), cut into florets
1 1/2 cups shredded low-fat Swiss cheese
   or cheddar cheese

Preheat the oven to 375°F.

   In a large skillet, heat the oil over medium-high heat. Add the onion, bell pepper, zucchini, and garlic and cook, stirring, for 5 to 7 minutes.

Helpful Hint:

To peel a butternut squash, first cut off the bell-shaped bottom and the top stem. Stand the cylinderlike part of the squash up on a cutting board; with a knife, cut down on the squash and peel off the thin skin. Rotate the squash as you go. Or, after cutting off the bottom and top, you can use a potato peeler to peel away the skin.

Transfer the vegetables to a 9 × 13–inch casserole dish or large Dutch oven. Stir in the water, quinoa, squash, parsley, salt, and pepper. Cover and bake for 25 minutes.

Remove the pan from the oven and stir in the broccoli. Bake until all of the liquid is absorbed, about 10 to 12 minutes more. Remove the casserole from the oven and fluff the quinoa and vegetables with a fork. Cover and let stand for about 10 minutes. When almost ready to serve, sprinkle the cheese evenly over the top and blend into the quinoa.

Makes *6* servings

Per Serving: 381 Calories; 13g Protein; 10g Fat; 52g Carbohydrates; 20mg Cholesterol; 453mg Sodium; 12g Fiber.

Thyme-Roasted Sunchokes

1¹/₂ tablespoons olive oil
2 teaspoons dried thyme or rosemary
¹/₂ teaspoon salt
¹/₂ teaspoon freshly ground black pepper
2 pounds sunchokes, or Jerusalem artichokes, scrubbed
    and halved lengthwise
4 to 6 cloves garlic
About ¹/₂ teaspoon paprika

Preheat the oven to 375°F.

Combine oil, thyme or rosemary, salt, and pepper in a mixing bowl. Toss in the sunchokes and coat well.

Place the garlic cloves and sunchokes cut-side down on a baking pan. Lightly sprinkle the paprika over the top. Place the pan in the oven and bake until the sunchokes are tender but not mushy, 35 to 45 minutes.

Transfer to a serving platter and cover. Keep warm until ready to serve. Serve sunchokes with pieces of roasted garlic.

Makes *6* servings

Per Serving: 150 Calories; 3g Protein; 3g Fat; 28g Carbohydrates; 0mg Cholesterol; 184mg Sodium; 3g Fiber.

Sweet Potato–Zucchini Muffins

2 large sweet potatoes, peeled
  and halved lengthwise
1/2 cup orange juice
1/2 cup canola oil
1/2 cup 1% or 2% milk, buttermilk,
  or rice milk
1 cup brown sugar, packed
1 large egg plus 1 large egg white

2 cups unbleached white flour
1 tablespoon baking powder
1 teaspoon salt
1 teaspoon ground cinnamon
1/2 teaspoon ground nutmeg
1 cup shredded zucchini
1 cup dark raisins or diced walnuts
Nonstick cooking spray

Helpful Hint:

To make pumpkin muffins, substitute about 2 cups of canned pumpkin for the mashed sweet potatoes.

Place the potatoes in boiling water to cover and cook over medium heat until tender, about 20 minutes. Cool under cold running water; drain. Transfer the potatoes to a bowl and mash with the back of a large spoon or potato masher. (There should be about 2 cups.)

Preheat the oven to 375°F.

In a mixing bowl, beat together the orange juice, oil, milk, brown sugar, egg, and egg white until creamy. Blend in the sweet potatoes.

In a separate bowl, mix together the flour, baking powder, salt, cinnamon, and nutmeg. Gently fold the dry ingredients into sweet potato batter. Fold in the zucchini and raisins or walnuts. Scoop the batter into lightly sprayed muffin tins and bake until a toothpick inserted in the center comes out clean, about 30 to 35 minutes. Remove the muffins from the oven and let cool on rack for about 15 minutes before wrapping or serving.

Makes *14* regular size or *6* to *8* large muffins

Per Regular Muffin: 376 Calories; 6g Protein; 9g Fat; 70g Carbohydrates; 16mg Cholesterol; 294mg Sodium; 5g Fiber.

Index

Page numbers in *italics* refer to photographs.

187